café@home

JULIE LE CLERC

café
@home

PHOTOGRAPHY BRUCE NICHOLSON

contents

ACKNOWLEDGEMENTS. I am forever grateful to have had the pleasure of working with my dream team whose combined talents have resulted in yet another brilliant book. I'd like to say a big thank you to Bruce Nicholson for creating strikingly memorable photographs that capture the essence of my food. I enjoy our knowledge exchange! Thanks to Grace Jones for seeing us through la vie en rose. Thank you Athena Sommerfeld for bringing everything together in a design that is both enticingly beautiful and practical. Thank you Bernice Beachman for sharing your wonderful sense of style, for the title, and for your vision of this book's shapeliness. And for opening your beautiful garden, house and cupboards of precious things for photography, I thank you once again. Thank you Philippa Gerrard for your brilliant editing skills and invaluable help in all sorts of ways. Thank you Helen Dixon for lending your composed hands and model's grace to these pages. Thanks to Loraine, Helen, Jo and Libby for tea-sets, a tea cosy or three, doilies and other delightful fripperies and props. Thanks to *Sunday Life* (Sydney and Melbourne), where some of these recipes first appeared. Many thanks to Michael Allpress and Allpress Espresso for making it your mission to expertly select, single batch roast and blend the world's best coffee beans for us to enjoy. We love your taste! And thanks to Jody, Russell and Geoff for making the espresso heroes illustrated in this book.

Grateful thanks go to these stores for kindly lending some of the beautiful tableware and accessories used as photographic props:
Nest. Kate Fitzpatrick for Cath Kidston fabrics. Madder and Rouge. Country Road Homeware. Sabato.

introduction

My greatest pleasure is to cook inviting food, and then to share this food with friends and family. There's nothing I enjoy more than being fully immersed in the process of creating and cooking recipes that provocatively engage all the senses. With this book, my desire is to present a style of food that reflects how I love to cook, and to illustrate some of the ways I like to entertain.

The book is a compilation of recipes of fashionable food popularised by modern café menus, rather than the food of any one café in particular. Daytime café food is smart, enticing, tasty, very adaptable and truly easy to reproduce in your own kitchen. Through the pages of this book, I reveal how to recreate the food and communal culture of a neighbourhood café @ home. I've used my knowledge as a chef and former café owner to formulate recipes that show just how simple café-style food is to cook at home. This is clever yet uncomplicated food, and a way of eating that we can all embrace.

From having owned several successful cafés and cooked in many professional kitchens, I know that for the home cook there is much to be learnt from café systems. My advice is to follow the lead of short-order chefs and use quality ingredients simply and well. Respect seasonal produce and focus on producing clean, clear flavours. The trick is to plan and prep a little in advance, and then any number of dishes can be achieved with ease. Some of these recipes will take a little time to prepare, but most are designed to produce good food fast, without jeopardising quality, taste or texture.

I find creating attractive settings for food extremely satisfying. I love to search shops for culinary-related items of beauty. Most of all, I love to use my own favourite belongings, such as new and old utensils, crockery, cutlery, cooking and serving bowls. It's silly to have these items sitting on display or hidden in a cupboard when using them gives so much pleasure. I encourage you to do the same, as you'll find visual presentation, as well as taste, is an important aspect of good food.

When I entertain in the daytime, I favour relaxed, informal table settings, though I always like to add a few nice touches to make each gathering extraordinary. With or without a special occasion to celebrate, I make each shared meal memorable by decorating the table or setting the scene in some way. I use colourful napkins, eclectic china, a posy of flowers from the garden, and meaningful arrangements of objets d'art to create ambience and express the individuality of each occasion. I don't own a formal tablecloth, but I do find that singularly interesting lengths of fabric lend themselves to this purpose beautifully so I either vaguely hem or fray the edges to good effect. And without fail I find that music is one of the most evocative ways to enhance the mood of a living space.

To make your daytime entertaining even easier, I've structured each chapter of *café@home* around recipes matched to different eating situations. For instance, I've created interesting morning food to enjoy in bed or to serve when friends come for brunch or a cup of coffee; clever ideas for an impromptu lunch; and pretty things to serve at a tea party in the afternoon. Some dishes are designed to be movable, so that they can be easily transported to outdoor eating situations. These movable feasts work just as well at home as they do for outdoor situations. For instance, plan a long, lazy picnic or simply a deliciously late lunch in your own garden. Take a weekend day-trip hamper to the beach or fire-up the backyard barbecue, make platters of salad and just relax.

Right now, brunch is my new favourite way to entertain friends. Mid-morning is a very relaxed hour, and all the pressures involved with hosting a dinner party, such as planning and serving different courses, thinking about wine matching, and so on, do not exist. I recommend brunch as the best weekend get-together meal and the most laid-back way to show hospitality. Brunch can be a help yourself kind of affair – serve platters of food that reflect the abundance of café counter-food or opt for loose, individual servings of simple morning treats. My advice is to stick to just one perfectly made, main 'dish of the day' such as Cinnamon Oat Pancakes or Home Baked Beans in Tomato Sauce. Another appealing

alternative is to move everything outdoors, gather everyone around small café tables and enjoy a food-to-go menu in the sunshine.

At home there are so many everyday entertaining options to choose from. One of my most adored treats has always been the charming ritual of afternoon tea. At a certain time in the afternoon, there's nothing more soothing than the chance to sit peacefully, to share a pot of tea and nibble a dainty titbit or two. This is when I find Louise Cake Tartlets or Orange Magdalenas are the perfect pick-me-up.

The morning coffee hour is a more lively time when the day's events can be planned over something delicious and an excellent shot of coffee to boost everyone's energy levels. To echo the intimacy of a café, I happily crowd a small lunch table with people, platters of food and copious amounts of scintillating conversation. For dessert, I serve great coffee and a selection of miniature sweets, as I find these are just the things to satiate a craving for a little sweetness. The possibilities for enjoying good food and friendship are endless.

Now, with the simplicity of café-style in mind, you can invite friends over any time and serve simply delicious, high-impact food in the seclusion of your own home.

Julie Le Clerc

quick conversions

weights

30g 1oz
125g 4oz
225g 8oz
450g .... 1 pound

measures

1 level teaspoon (universal) 5ml
1 level tablespoon (NZ, UK, US) 15ml
1 level tablespoon (Australia) 20ml
1 cup liquid 250ml
4 cups liquid .... 1 litre
1 pint 600ml

useful equivalents

1 egg white 30g
1 level cup flour 150g
1 level cup sugar 200g

oven temperature guide

Description	°C	°F	Gas Mark
Slow	110–130	225–250	½–1
Moderately slow	140–160	275–325	2–3
Moderate	180–190	350–375	4–5
Moderately hot	190–200	375–400	5–6
Hot	210–240	425–450	7–8
Very hot	250–260	475–500	9–10

As oven models and thermostats vary, these conversions are a guide only. Fan-forced ovens (convection ovens) are usually set lower than conventional ovens. Increase the fan-forced temperature given by 10–20° for conventional ovens or refer to the manufacturer's instructions.

01. bre

akfast
in bed

Lazy weekend mornings. Eating breakfast while snuggled under the covers. Delicious feelings of stolen time. Luxuriate in the cosy comfort of your own nest.

toasted cranberry and pistachio granola

The beauty of mixing and toasting your own granola (muesli) is that you can add, subtract or substitute ingredients as you please to create your own signature blend.

2 tablespoons olive oil
1 cup whole oats
1 cup rolled oats
1/2 cup wheatgerm
1/2 cup desiccated coconut threads
1/4 cup sunflower seeds
1/4 cup linseeds
1/2 cup liquid honey
1/2 cup shelled pistachio nuts
1/2 cup dried cranberries (or substitute raisins)
1/2 cup dried small figs, halved

1 Preheat oven to 175°C. Grease an oven pan with the olive oil and place the next six dry ingredients in the pan. Drizzle with honey and stir to combine.
2 Bake for 20 minutes, stirring regularly, until ingredients are toasted to golden brown. Remove pan from the oven to cool, then stir in pistachio nuts, dried cranberries and figs. Store in an airtight container.
3 Serve with milk or yoghurt.

Makes 5 cups

+ my advice ... it is best not to toast pistachio nuts for this mix as they will discolour. The bright splash of green is so pretty and raw nuts are good for your health.

maple-roasted stone fruits with raspberry crush sauce

I find these roasted fruits last for several days stored in the fridge, and they just taste better and better.

4–6 pieces of stone fruit of choice, such as apricots, peaches, nectarines, plums, cherries
15g butter, cut into small cubes
1/4 cup maple syrup
icing sugar to dust

1 Preheat oven to 200°C. Halve fruit and remove stones. Place in an oven pan, dot with butter and drizzle with maple syrup. Roast for 15–20 minutes until fruit is caramelised and golden brown.
2 Serve fruit dusted with icing sugar and drizzled with raspberry crush sauce.

Serves 2

raspberry crush sauce

1 cup sugar
1/4 cup water
juice of 3 lemons
300g raspberries (fresh or frozen)

1 Place sugar, water and lemon juice in a saucepan and bring to the boil, stirring until sugar has dissolved, then simmer for 2–3 minutes.
2 Add raspberries and lightly crush. Simmer for 3–5 minutes until mixture is syrupy, though not as thick as jam. Serve with roasted stone fruit.

Makes 1 cup

+ this goes with that ... for a quick dessert, serve hot raspberry crush sauce over ice-cream, Greek yoghurt or any small cakes.

peach pikelets

Serve these fruity pikelets with extra fresh fruit on the side or go with tradition and serve them topped with lashings of jam and whipped or clotted cream.

1¹/2 cups plain flour

3 tablespoons caster sugar

1 teaspoon bicarbonate of soda (baking soda)

2 teaspoons cream of tartar

pinch salt

1 tablespoon melted butter

1 egg

1 cup milk

2 fresh peaches, halved and stones removed

oil for frying

1 Place dry ingredients in a bowl. Add melted butter, egg and milk and whisk to combine into a smooth batter. Thinly slice peaches.

2 Heat a large non-stick frying pan, add a little oil and some peach slices, then top each peach slice with a good tablespoonful of batter. Cook over a moderate heat for 1–2 minutes on each side until golden.

Makes 16

+ substitute ... any other sliced stone fruit in summer, such as nectarines, apricots or plums. Or try thin slices of apple or pear in the wintertime.

bircher muesli

Bircher muesli is a creamy, moist, raw, fruit-filled mix, invented by Swiss nutritionist, Dr Bircher-Brenner.

1 cup rolled oats

¹/2 cup desiccated coconut threads

1 cup fresh orange juice

juice of 1 lemon

¹/4 cup liquid honey

1 cup thick plain yoghurt

2 bananas, mashed

1 apple, grated

8 fresh apricots, stones removed and chopped (or other seasonal fruit, such as fresh berries)

¹/4 cup chopped nuts, such as almonds, pecans or pistachio nuts

1 Place oats and coconut in a bowl and pour over fruit juices. Cover and refrigerate overnight.

2 Next morning, mix in honey, yoghurt and fruit. Serve topped with chopped nuts.

Serves 4

+ serving suggestion ... fill a big glass bowl with Bircher muesli and top with extra fresh fruit salad – try cut strawberries, papaya, and summer stone fruit, folded together with passionfruit pulp. Arrange small bowls of toasted nuts, seeds and dried fruit for each person to sprinkle over their individual serving.

banana berry buttermilk smoothie

A powerful smoothie might be all you need to start the day. Add a tablespoon of wheatgerm for extra nutritive value.

2 bananas

1 cup fresh or frozen berries

½ cup crushed ice

2–3 tablespoons honey

1 cup buttermilk

1 Place all ingredients in a blender or food processor and blend until smooth, adding honey to sweeten to taste.
2 Pour into cold glasses and serve with straws.

Serves 2

pear and rhubarb yoghurt smoothie

Pear and rhubarb give a nice textural component to this smoothie.

1 cup roughly chopped rhubarb

¼ cup cold water

1 pear, peeled, cored and roughly chopped

½ cup crushed ice

1 cup thick plain yoghurt

2–3 tablespoons honey

1 Place rhubarb in a saucepan with cold water. Cover and cook over a gentle heat for 5 minutes or until rhubarb is tender. Remove to cool.
2 Place cold rhubarb and remaining ingredients in a blender or food processor and blend until smooth, adding honey to taste. Chill well.
3 Pour into cold glasses and serve with straws.

Serves 2

+ substitute ... milk, yoghurt, soy milk, buttermilk, goats' milk, almond milk and coconut milk are all interchangeable components in a smoothie mix.

mango and coconut milk whip

Deliciously fragrant and sweet, mangoes form a decadent fruit base to this rich whip.

2 fresh mangoes, peeled and flesh cut from the stones

½ cup crushed ice

400ml can coconut milk

sugar to taste

1 Place all ingredients in a blender or food processor and blend until smooth, adding sugar to sweeten to taste.
2 Pour into cold glasses and serve with straws.

Serves 2

chocolate banana bread

Chocolate banana bread is delicious as is, or try it toasted and spread with butter.

150g butter

3/4 cup caster sugar

2 eggs

2 tablespoons milk

2 ripe bananas, thickly sliced

1 cup self-raising flour

1 teaspoon bicarbonate of soda (baking soda)

1/4 cup Dutch process cocoa powder

1/2 cup chocolate chips

1 Preheat oven to 180°C on fan-bake. Grease and flour an 11 x 25 x 7cm loaf tin.

2 With an electric mixer, cream butter and sugar together until pale. Beat in eggs, milk and sliced bananas.

3 Stir in sifted dry ingredients to combine. Lastly, stir in chocolate chips. Spoon mixture into the loaf tin and bake for 45 minutes or until a skewer inserted comes out clean. Turn out onto a wire rack to cool. Slice to serve.

4 Loaf will last 3–4 days if stored in an airtight container.

Makes 1 loaf

+ Dutch cocoa powder undergoes a process to neutralise its acidity. The result is a finer, deeper-coloured powder with a mellow cocoa taste. These superior differences are noticeable when Dutch process cocoa is used in baking.

vanilla cherry jam with toast

Home-made jam that incorporates lots of fresh fruit is so magnificent that you just want to eat it by the spoonful.

1kg black cherries, stoned

1 vanilla bean, split in half

5 cups sugar

juice of 1 lemon

1 teaspoon pectin (available from supermarkets or health food stores)

toasted bread of choice

1 Place all jam ingredients into a preserving pan or large saucepan. Slowly bring to the boil, stirring until sugar has dissolved.

2 Simmer for 10–15 minutes or until setting point is reached. Test for setting point by placing a teaspoonful of jam on a chilled plate. If the sample wrinkles when pushed with a finger, the jam is ready to set.

3 Skim any foam from the surface of the jam. Remove from heat to cool for 10 minutes, then stir so that the fruit will be evenly distributed.

4 Ladle into hot sterilised jars (sterilise jars in a 150°C oven for 30 minutes) and seal well. Serve with toast.

Makes about 6 cups

+ this goes with that ... incorporate vanilla cherry jam in a sweet French toast sandwich (see page 39).

toasted bagel with avocado and two pestos

Serve toasted bagels with slices of fresh, buttery-textured avocado and a little of each flavourful pesto on the side.

green pesto

Cashew nuts give this pesto an extra luscious and creamy texture. It's the lemon juice that maintains the vibrant, herbal green colour and lends a refreshing quality to the taste.

1 cup parsley leaves, tightly packed

¼ cup mint leaves

¼ cup basil leaves

½ cup lemon juice

½ cup cashew nut pieces

¼–½ cup extra virgin olive oil

sea salt and freshly ground black pepper

1 Place parsley, mint and basil leaves and lemon juice in the bowl of a food processor and process to chop.
2 Add cashew nuts and process until well blended. With the motor running, drizzle in enough olive oil to form a smooth paste. Season with salt and pepper to taste.

Makes about 2 cups

red pesto

Based on the concept that pesto is essentially a ground paste, this is a vivid red blend that can be used as a dip or spread.

2 cloves garlic, peeled

¼ cup basil leaves

3 red peppers, seeds removed and roasted

½ cup sun-dried tomatoes, roughly chopped

¼ cup tomato paste

1 teaspoon sugar

¼ cup extra virgin olive oil

sea salt and freshly ground black pepper

1 Place garlic in the bowl of a food processor and pulse to chop. Add basil, red peppers, sun-dried tomatoes, tomato paste and sugar. Process to purée.
2 With the motor running, drizzle in enough olive oil to form a smooth paste. Season with salt and pepper to taste.

Makes about 2 cups

+ this goes with that ... spread green pesto in ribbon tea sandwiches (see page 147); incorporate red pesto in asparagus and red pesto chicken rolls (see page 82).

+ bagels ... are speciality breads shaped with a hole in the centre. Real bagels are fat-free and low in sugar. The characteristic chewy texture of bagels is due to the fact that they are boiled before baking or baked with moist heat.

+ my advice … remove the core, seeds and white membranes from peppers before roasting them. Place halved red peppers in an oven pan, rub with a little olive oil and roast at 200°C for 30 minutes, or until the skins blister and the flesh is soft. Remove to a bowl and cover with plastic wrap so that the peppers sweat and the skins loosen. Once cool enough to handle, the skins can easily be slipped off.

fruit pastries

Reflect the seasons with different fruit toppings.
Try sliced banana, pineapple, mango or stone
fruit in summer, or poached quince, pear or
apple in winter.

1 pre-rolled sheet puff pastry

1 egg

1 tablespoon cream

finely grated zest of 1 orange

2 tablespoons sugar

4 fresh figs, sliced, or other seasonal fruit of choice, such
    as sliced apples, pears, stone fruit or berries

1 Preheat oven to 200°C. Divide the pastry sheet into 4
even squares and place on a lightly oiled baking tray. Prick
pastry all over with a fork and brush with a mixture of egg
lightly beaten with the cream.
2 Combine orange zest and sugar and sprinkle half this mix
over pastry squares, leaving a 2cm border on all sides.
Arrange chosen fruit in the centre of each square and top
with remaining zest and sugar mix.
3 Bake for 20 minutes or until the pastry edges are puffed
and golden brown. Pastries are best eaten while still warm.

Makes 4

+ shortcut ... frozen, pre-
rolled sheets of pastry are
a convenient product to have
on hand. Leave sheets whole
to make a bigger tart or cut
to required size, cover with
chosen sweet or savoury
topping and bake.

kedgeree

This is a traditional, Indian-influenced, English breakfast dish. If it makes your life easier, the rice can be cooked the day before and the fish flaked, ready for a quick morning cook-up.

2 cups basmati or long-grain rice

50g butter

1 onion, finely sliced

2 teaspoons medium-hot curry powder

2 bay leaves

1/2 cup milk, or fish stock if preferred

200g smoked fish, flaked

small bunch spring onions, sliced

3 tablespoons chopped parsley

zest and juice of 1 lemon

3 hard-boiled eggs, peeled and quartered

sea salt and freshly ground black pepper

1 Cook rice in plenty of boiling salted water for 12 minutes, at a rolling boil, until tender, then drain well.
2 Melt butter in a saucepan, add onion and cook for 5 minutes over a medium heat until golden. Add curry powder, bay leaves and milk (or stock) and bring to the boil. Add cooked rice, flaked smoked fish, spring onions, parsley, lemon zest and juice, and stir-fry until mixture is hot.
3 Season to taste with salt and pepper and serve garnished with egg quarters.

Serves 4

+ my advice ... soft-boil eggs by placing them in a saucepan of boiling water and cooking for 3 minutes (the egg white will be just cooked and the yolk runny) or 4 minutes for slightly more set egg white but still runny yolk. Hard-boil eggs for 7 minutes. Over-cooking will result in a dark-coloured ring around the yolks.

coddled eggs with parsley and garlic toast

Coddling is an old-fashioned method used to gently cook eggs in a container – if you don't have special egg coddlers, use ramekins tightly covered with foil.

1 teaspoon butter

1 tablespoon cream

2 eggs

sea salt and freshly ground black pepper

parsley and garlic toast

2 tablespoons softened butter

1 clove garlic, crushed

2 tablespoons finely chopped parsley

4 slices wholegrain toast

1 Place half the butter and cream in each of two ramekins or special egg coddlers. Break eggs into ramekins. Season with salt and pepper and tightly cover ramekin with foil or place lid on coddlers.
2 Place ramekins in a large saucepan and fill with boiling water to come half-way up the sides of the ramekins. Cook eggs in this water bath at a gentle simmer for 4–5 minutes for soft eggs. Remove covering and serve in the cooking vessel with toast spread with parsley and garlic butter.
3 To make parsley and garlic toast, combine butter, garlic and parsley in a bowl and beat until creamy. Spread on toast and cut into fingers (soldiers).

Serves 2

+ flavour options ... add some freshly chopped herbs such as basil, chives, parsley, tarragon or marjoram to the eggs before coddling, or add a small amount of finely chopped mushrooms, or top coddled eggs with a dollop of pesto.

+ how to ... test eggs for freshness: place eggs in a bowl of cold water – fresh eggs will fall to the bottom; stale eggs will float near the surface.

mushroom-baked brioches

These mushroom-bakes are like savoury bread and butter puddings – they're meltingly soft and luscious to eat.

4 large field mushrooms

1 tablespoon balsamic vinegar

2 tablespoons chopped fresh oregano

sea salt and freshly ground black pepper

4 stale individual brioches, or substitute small, soft bread rolls

3 large eggs

2 cups milk

1/4 cup cream

1 Very finely chop the mushrooms with a knife or in a food processor. Blend in balsamic vinegar, oregano and season well with salt and pepper to taste.

2 Slice brioches or bread rolls into 4 layers. Spread mushroom paste between each layer, then sandwich back together. Place into four, small, deep, ovenproof dishes to fit compactly.

3 Beat eggs, milk and cream together, season well and pour evenly over brioches. Leave to rest for 30 minutes (or overnight) until bread has absorbed the liquid.

4 Preheat oven to 150°C on fan-bake. Bake for 20–25 minutes or until custard is just set. Serve immediately.

Serves 4

+ substitute ... this mushroom filling can be replaced with any flavouring you fancy. For instance, try adding chopped bacon or ham, or substitute puréed spinach.

croque-monsieur

Basically, this is the French version of a toasted ham and Gruyère cheese sandwich. They're typical fare of French bars. Use the best quality bread, cheese and ham, and make yourself a slice of heaven.

1/2 cup milk

1 bay leaf

1 tablespoon butter

1 teaspoon wholegrain mustard

2 teaspoons standard flour

sea salt and freshly ground black pepper

25g butter to spread on bread

4 slices quality bread

100g sliced ham off the bone

100g Gruyère cheese, grated

1 Place the milk and bay leaf in a saucepan and bring to the boil, then remove from the heat and set aside for the milk to infuse with the flavour of the bay leaf. Make a roux by melting the butter and mustard in a saucepan over a low heat. Stir in the flour to form a smooth paste and simmer, stirring constantly for 1 minute to cook the flour. Strain the infused milk and discard the bay leaf. Add the milk to the roux and stir to combine. Return the saucepan to the heat and cook, stirring constantly until the sauce thickens. Season with salt and pepper to taste and remove to cool.

2 Spread the slices of bread with the butter and turn the slices upside-down. Now spread the up-turned side of 2 slices with the white sauce. Top the sauce with some sliced ham and then grated cheese. Place the remaining 2 slices on top to form sandwiches, with the butter on the outside.

3 Heat a frying pan over a medium heat and fry the sandwiches until the cheese melts and the bread is golden brown on both sides.

Makes 2

+ flavour options ... croque-madame is another version of this French classic, where a poached or fried egg is included in the filling.

unch
with friends

Set a table in the morning sun. Serve short-order feasts from your own kitchen. Sensational produce – simply cooked. Revitalising tastes shared with friends.

fruit bruschetta with verjuice-poached rhubarb

Brunch is such a nice way to entertain. The food you serve can be as simple as bruschetta with special toppings. It's getting together with friends in a relaxed way that's important.

1¹⁄₂ cups verjuice

1 cup sugar

4 stalks rhubarb, cut into 4cm lengths

4 slices fruit bread

150g ricotta, quark or cream cheese

1 Place verjuice and sugar in a saucepan and bring to the boil, stirring until sugar dissolves. Boil for 2–3 minutes, then lower heat to barely simmer – the liquid should hardly tremble. Add the rhubarb and leave to poach for 5 minutes so that the rhubarb holds its shape. Do not boil as this will cause the rhubarb to break up. Remove to a deep-sided flat dish to cool in the poaching liquid.

2 Slice fruit bread and char-grill or toast. Spread with ricotta, quark or cream cheese, top with pieces of rhubarb and drizzle with syrup.

Serves 4

+ verjuice (*verjus* in French) is the unfermented juice of unripe grapes. It can be used in place of wine or vinegar in cooking, dressings and marinades. Verjuice is less acidic than vinegar and more acidic than wine, so to incorporate verjuice, adjust recipe proportions to taste.

fresh apple crush

Use a high-powered blender to pulverise whole apples and ice into sweet, green apple slush.

Per person:

1 green apple

juice of 1 lemon

1 cup crushed ice

sugar to taste

1 Remove core from apple. Roughly chop apple. Leave the skin on the apple to add its colour to the drink.

2 Place all ingredients in a blender and purée to form an icy drink.

Serves 1

melonade

This is the prettiest homemade lemonade with a twist: the addition of crushed melon tinged with mint.

1kg pink watermelon, rock melon or honey dew melon
   flesh, seeds removed and chopped

juice of 10 lemons

1 cup mineral water (use sparkling mineral water if desired)

1 cup sugar

3 sprigs fresh mint leaves

1 Place melon, lemon juice, mineral water and sugar in a blender and purée to form a textured drink. This may need to be done in 3 batches

2 Chill well and serve with floating mint leaves.

Serves 8

cinnamon oat pancakes with maple bananas

My sister Helen introduced me to this great recipe when we were setting up our first café. These pancakes ended up on the café menu and became wildly popular. I've cooked a fair number in my time and they're still a favourite when I have friends to brunch.

1 cup rolled oats

1 cup milk

3 tablespoons sugar

2 tablespoons fruity extra virgin olive oil

1 egg, lightly beaten

½ cup plain flour

2 teaspoons baking powder

1 teaspoon cinnamon

½ teaspoon salt

1–2 tablespoons extra milk if required

4 bananas, peeled and sliced

vegetable oil

maple syrup and yoghurt to serve

1 Place the oats in a bowl, cover with milk and set aside to soak for 10 minutes. Add sugar, oil and egg and stir to combine. Stir in sifted remaining dry ingredients to form a smooth batter. Add a little extra milk to thin if necessary.

2 In a large, non-stick frying pan over a medium heat, cook big spoonfuls of the mixture in a little oil for 2 minutes on each side, turning once, until golden brown. You will have 8 pancakes. This will need to be done in batches, but keep pancakes warm in a moderate oven until you have cooked them all.

3 Serve bananas between pancakes with plenty of maple syrup and yoghurt if desired.

Serves 4

+ shortcut ... the pancake mixture can be prepped-up the night before and tossed to order when desired. If you're cooking for a big group of friends or family, the best good cook's tip I can recommend is to get everyone to toss their own pancakes!

sweet french toast sandwich

The advantage of a late starting time for brunch means that there is not only time to dawdle over eating but also time to enjoy the process of cooking something special.

8 thick slices bread (preferably fruit or brioche loaf)

8 tablespoons ricotta

4 tablespoons fruity jam (try vanilla cherry jam, see page 21)

2 eggs

½ cup milk

1 tablespoon caster sugar

oil for frying

1 Lay 4 slices of bread on a work surface. Spread each slice with ricotta, followed by a layer of jam and top with a second slice of bread. Press together firmly.
2 In a bowl whisk eggs with milk and sugar. Heat a non-stick frying pan and add a little oil. Dip sandwiches into egg mixture briefly, then fry for 1–2 minutes on each side over a medium-low heat until golden brown. Serve immediately.

Makes 4

+ my advice ... the secret to success with this French toast variant is to quickly dip the sandwiches in the wet mixture, just enough to moisten the bread.

espresso frappé

I first enjoyed this refreshing non-dairy drink in a small Greek Island town. Milk can be added if desired, but it is not really necessary.

Per person:

1 cup crushed ice

1 double espresso coffee

sugar to taste

1 Place the crushed ice in a blender. Pour over the hot espresso and blend to form an icy drink, adding sugar to taste if desired.
2 Serve in a tall glass with a straw.

Serves 1

+ my advice ... greet your guests with a delicious, long cold drink such as a frappé, melonade or crush and then the pressure is off. Make individual espresso coffees for a small group, but for a crowd opt for ease and go with plunger coffee.

sticky black rice with fresh fruit

I find this a brilliant dish to serve when I'm entertaining friends for brunch. The rice can be cooked several days in advance and stored in the fridge until needed. Sticky black rice also makes a divine dessert to serve after a spicy Asian-inspired meal.

1½ cups black glutinous rice

2 litres cold water

3 pandan leaves or substitute 2 stalks lemongrass, lightly crushed

200g palm sugar, shaved, or substitute brown sugar

300ml can coconut cream

1 fresh mango, sliced or other fresh fruit of choice

1 Rinse the rice 3 times in cold water and drain well. Place the rice and measured cold water in a large saucepan and bring to the boil. Add the pandan leaves or lemongrass and lower the heat to simmer, uncovered, for 1 hour, stirring regularly until the rice is soft and the cooking liquid has reduced and thickened.

2 Remove the pandan leaves or lemongrass and stir in the palm sugar. Transfer to a bowl to cool.

3 Meanwhile, simmer the coconut cream in a small saucepan for 10 minutes to thicken. Remove to a bowl to cool.

4 Serve the rice with fresh mango and a good drizzle of thick coconut cream.

Serves 4

+ palm sugar is sugar gained from the sap of various palms. It comes in hard blocks, and needs to be crushed or grated before use. There are dark and light varieties of palm sugar. Pandan leaves are available from Asian grocery stores – I buy them from the freezer section, frozen in bundles.

stewed mixed peppers with scrambled eggs and chives

Cooked in this way, the multi-coloured peppers melt together. Combined with the bite of salty capers and some great scrambled eggs – brunch doesn't get much better than this!

1 each red, yellow and orange peppers
¼ cup olive oil
¼ cup capers
sea salt and freshly ground black pepper

scrambled eggs

6 eggs
½ cup cream
sea salt and freshly ground black pepper
25g butter
3 tablespoons snipped fresh chives or chopped
   fresh parsley
4–8 slices ciabatta bread, toasted

1 Remove stems, seeds and white membrane from all peppers. Cut flesh into thin strips.
2 Heat a pan, add oil and sliced peppers and cook over a gentle heat for 15 minutes until softened, adding a little water if necessary to stop peppers from sticking to the pan. Add capers, season with salt and pepper to taste and serve with scrambled eggs and toasted ciabatta bread.
3 To scramble eggs, place eggs and cream in a bowl and whisk lightly to combine. Season well with salt and pepper. Heat a non-stick pan, add butter to melt and then pour in egg mixture and cook over a medium heat. As the egg sets around the edges, draw the set egg into the centre of the pan with a wooden spoon. Repeat until egg mixture is mostly set but still a little moist. Scatter with chives or parsley to serve.

Serves 4

+ serving suggestion ... when I'm entertaining on a balmy summer's morning I like to serve brunch outside. Arrange everything in big bowls or platters and let people serve themselves over relaxed conversation.

eggs florentine

Spinach and eggs are a classic combination, proving that good things never lose their appeal!

hollandaise sauce

¼ cup white wine vinegar
150g butter
3 egg yolks, at room temperature
2 teaspoons lemon juice
sea salt

4–8 eggs (1–2 per person)
4 split English muffins or bagels
2 cups baby spinach leaves, blanched for 20 seconds
   in boiling water and drained well
freshly ground black pepper

1 To make the Hollandaise sauce, in a small saucepan simmer vinegar until reduced by half. In another saucepan heat butter to melt but do not boil, then cool to blood heat.
2 Place egg yolks, lemon juice and ½ teaspoon salt in the bowl of a food processor or a mixing bowl. Process or whisk until frothy and pale. With the motor running or while whisking vigorously and continuously, pour on the butter in a thin and steady stream alternately with reduced vinegar. A thick, creamy sauce will form – avoid using the milky whey that separates out from the butter as this will thin the sauce. Adjust seasoning with salt if necessary. Use immediately or keep warm.
3 Soft poach eggs in a pan of simmering water. Toast muffins or bagels.
4 To assemble, place hot blanched spinach on toasted muffins, top with well-drained poached eggs, smother with Hollandaise sauce and season with pepper.

Serves 4

+ substitute ... if ham or bacon is used instead of spinach then this dish is called Eggs Benedict. Smoked salmon is a tasty substitute or addition to the spinach. Another vegetarian option is steamed asparagus when in season.

turkish breakfast platter

For good brunch flavours it is possible to embrace all kinds of food traditions and introduce them to the morning routine.

250g feta cheese, cubed

2 cups quality black olives

8 sliced vine-ripened tomatoes

pide (Turkish flat bread), sliced

small bowl filled with extra virgin olive oil

1 Arrange all ingredients on a large platter so that eaters can help themselves.
2 Eat by dipping bread in the oil and topping with other ingredients to taste.

Serves 4

+ good idea ... brunch is the new dinner party! Invite friends to brunch and enjoy socialising in a relaxed morning environment. Preparing brunch is less of a performance than giving a dinner party, and you only need to serve one course (or two if you're in the mood). It's the perfect way to entertain.

italian sausages with tomato jam

I'm not keen on the mass fry-up type of all-day breakfast plate. It's a palaver to prepare for a crowd and too huge to appreciate. I think a quality, single item cooked to perfection (such as excellent sausages) is a greater triumph.

tomato jam

1 onion, finely chopped

400g can chopped tomatoes

½ cup raw sugar

½ cup red wine vinegar

2 tablespoons olive oil

½ teaspoon chilli flakes

½ teaspoon sea salt

pinch allspice powder

8 coarse-textured, Italian-style sausages (usually flavoured with fennel seeds)

1 To make the tomato jam, place all ingredients except sausages in a saucepan and bring to the boil, stirring until sugar dissolves. Simmer gently for about 10 minutes or until thick and jammy. Store in the fridge.
2 Place sausages in a non-stick frying pan with enough cold water to fill the pan to 5mm. Place the pan over a high heat and cook, turning the sausages until the water has evaporated. Continue cooking and turning sausages until they are browned all over. Serve with tomato jam.

Serves 4

feta, corn and spring onion fritters with crisp prosciutto

Fritters are an all-time childhood favourite for many people. I recommend serving these tasty fritters for brunch, lunch or even as a light supper dish.

3/4 cup plain flour, sifted

1 teaspoon baking powder

4 spring onions, finely chopped

150g feta cheese, crumbled

2 tablespoons chopped fresh parsley

440g can cream-style corn

1 egg, lightly beaten

sea salt and freshly ground black pepper

oil for frying

8 slices prosciutto

1 Combine flour, baking powder, spring onions, feta and parsley in a bowl. Stir in corn and beaten egg to form a batter. Season with salt and pepper to taste.

2 Heat a large, non-stick frying pan. Add a little oil and fry tablespoonful lots of batter in batches over a medium heat until golden brown on both sides, turning once. Drain on paper towels. Fry prosciutto for about 30 seconds only as it will crisp very quickly.

3 Layer fritters with prosciutto and serve with a favourite chutney on the side, or try my tomato jam (see page 44).

Serves 4

+ my advice ... fry fritters over a medium heat as they take time to cook through to the centre. If the heat source is too high the centre of the fritters will still be raw when the surface has blackened.

balsamic mushrooms on toast

If the field mushrooms have any remnants of soil clinging to them, simply brush this off with a dry paper towel. I recommend mushrooms be stored in a paper bag in the fridge to protect them from deterioration.

500g large field mushrooms

2 tablespoons olive oil

1 tablespoon aged balsamic vinegar

1/2 cup cream

sea salt and freshly ground black pepper

4 bagels, halved and toasted or 8 slices toast

2 tablespoons chopped fresh parsley

1 Thickly slice mushrooms or leave whole if preferred. Heat a frying pan, add oil and mushrooms and stir-fry for 3–5 minutes to lightly brown. Add balsamic vinegar and cook briefly, then add cream. Simmer for a few minutes to reduce and thicken cream sauce. Season with salt and pepper to taste.

2 Spoon over toast or toasted bagels, sprinkle with parsley and serve immediately.

Serves 4

+ this goes with that ... this mushroom mixture is the base to many meal possibilities, for instance, layer sheets of lasagne with balsamic mushrooms and bake; serve balsamic mushrooms as a sauce over grilled steak or chicken breasts; or purée balsamic mushrooms with enough chicken stock to create an earthy mushroom soup.

home-baked beans in tomato sauce

This rustic bean dish is the perfect brunch meal to make in advance, as its flavours only improve upon sitting. Serve home-baked beans with crusty bread to mop up the rich tomato sauce.

250g cannellini beans

200g pancetta, in one piece, or 1 pork hock

2 x 400g cans chopped tomatoes

4 cloves garlic, chopped

1 large onion, peeled and chopped

1 tablespoon wholegrain mustard

3 tablespoons brown sugar

3 tablespoons Worcestershire sauce

2 tablespoons olive oil

2 tablespoons chopped fresh marjoram or oregano

sea salt and freshly ground black pepper

1 Place beans in a bowl, cover with plenty of cold water and leave to soak overnight. Next day, drain beans well and place them in a saucepan with plenty of fresh cold water. Bring to the boil, then simmer for 40 minutes until beans are just tender. Drain beans, discarding the cooking liquid.

2 Preheat oven to 180°C. In a large ovenproof casserole dish, combine drained beans with the remaining ingredients, except salt and pepper.

3 Cover and bake for 2 hours, stirring beans up from the bottom once or twice during cooking. Season with salt and pepper to taste.

Serves 4

+ my advice ... dried beans need to be soaked overnight in cold water to soften them and shorten their cooking time. It is important to discard the soaking water because it can contain impurities. Cook beans in plenty of fresh water, as they swell in size during cooking. Do not salt the cooking water – this will cause beans to toughen – but do season the completed dish.

+ good idea ... buy tomatoes on the vine and leave them in a bowl to continue to ripen and improve in flavour. Avoid refrigerating tomatoes as the cold causes them to lose their flavour and become watery or powdery in texture.

+ my advice ... choose a type of potato with qualities that suit the style of dish you are cooking. Some potatoes cook to a floury texture and these are perfect for mashing, roasting, baking in their jackets and making potato gnocchi. Other potatoes cook to a waxy texture and these are good for steaming, salads, casseroles, deep-frying, and for dishes where you need the spuds to hold together, such as a gratin or hash browns. Ask your greengrocer's advice if potatoes are not labelled.

hash browns with pastrami and roast tomatoes

Inviting friends for brunch is much less pressured than hosting a dinner party, and these hash browns are a great one-course meal to serve mid-morning.

800g (4 large) waxy or all-purpose potatoes, peeled
¼ cup chopped fresh parsley
2 tablespoons sour cream
1 tablespoon horseradish cream
sea salt and freshly ground black pepper
12 small tomatoes on the vine
olive oil for frying
8 slices pastrami

1 Cook the potatoes whole in boiling salted water for 10 minutes. Drain and dry potatoes and then coarsely grate into a bowl. Mix in parsley, sour cream and horseradish cream, and season well with salt and pepper.
2 Preheat oven to 200°C. Place tomatoes in an oven pan and drizzle with a little olive oil and season with salt and pepper. Bake for 10–15 minutes until starting to brown.
3 Heat a non-stick frying pan, add a little oil and cook compressed handfuls of the potato mixture over a medium heat for 3–4 minutes until crisp and golden brown. Turn over and cook the other side. Remove to paper towels to drain. This will need to be done in batches, but hash browns can be kept warm with the tomatoes for a short while in the hot oven.
4 In the same frying pan, add a little oil and cook pastrami as you would bacon, for 30 seconds on each side until golden brown. Serve hash browns with pastrami and tomatoes.

Serves 4

rning
coffee

Take a well-deserved break. Enjoy
excellent coffee and a savoury or
sweet home-baked treat. Experience
café culture in the comfort of your
own home.

+ coffee speak … a short black espresso is made with
a single shot of espresso extracted to 30mls and served
in a very small glass or cup (called a *demi-tasse*).
Traditionally, white sugar is added to taste.

iced coffee

If you have a home coffee machine, make espresso coffee; otherwise good, strong, plunger coffee works well as a base for iced coffee.

Per person:

1 double shot espresso

3/4 cup milk

2 tablespoons whipped cream

1 scoop vanilla ice-cream (optional)

1 tablespoon grated chocolate

1 Combine espresso and milk in a tall glass and chill well.

2 Top iced coffee with whipped cream (and ice-cream if desired) and sprinkle with grated chocolate. Serve with a long spoon and a straw.

Serves 1

spiced liquid hot chocolate

Use the best chocolate you can afford for cooking, for eating and in this case, for drinking.

Per person:

100g quality dark chocolate, chopped

3/4 cup milk

1 cinnamon stick

1 Melt chocolate carefully over a pan of simmering water or in the microwave. Heat milk and cinnamon stick together in a pan until hot but not boiling. Leave briefly to infuse.

2 Pour hot milk over melted chocolate, whisking to blend. Pour into a cup or mug to serve.

Serves 1

+ my advice ... melting chocolate is a delicate process. The best way to melt chocolate is to place chopped chocolate in a bowl set over simmering water, gently stirring until melted and smooth. Or carefully melt in a microwave oven using short bursts at a medium-low power level, stopping to stir between bursts.

almond croissants

Symbolic of dreamy holidays spent in France, almond croissants are a deliciously clever way to revive day-old croissants, disguised as a decadent pastry creation.

almond cream

65g butter, softened

1/4 cup caster sugar

1 egg

1 drop almond essence (optional)

3/4 cup ground almonds

1 tablespoon plain flour

6 croissants (day-old croissants are fine)

1/4 cup flaked (sliced) almonds

1 To make the almond cream, beat butter and sugar in a bowl with an electric mixer until pale and creamy. Beat in egg and almond essence. Stir in ground almonds and flour.
2 Heat oven to 180°C. Slice croissants in half. Lay bottom half of each croissant on a baking tray and slather with almond cream. Replace croissant tops and spread with a little almond cream. Scatter with flaked almonds. Bake for 10–15 minutes until golden.

Makes 6

+ my advice ... store ground and whole nuts, and nut oils, in the fridge to protect them from heat, which can cause them to deteriorate and turn rancid.

lemon sugar and sweet basil cup-cakes

Basil may seem a strange herb to include in a sweet, baked item, but believe me it works well and contributes a pleasant fragrance and slightly aniseed taste to these sugary morning cup-cakes.

125g butter

3/4 cup sugar

finely grated zest of 1 lemon

3 eggs

1/2 cup sour cream

1/4 cup finely shredded basil leaves

1 cup plain flour

1 teaspoon baking powder

lemon sugar

finely grated zest of 1 lemon

juice of 3 lemons

1/2 cup caster sugar

1 Preheat oven to 175°C on fan-bake. Grease and flour a 12-hole, standard muffin pan.
2 Beat butter and sugar in a bowl until pale and creamy. Beat in lemon zest and eggs, then fold in sour cream and shredded basil. Fold in sifted dry ingredients. Spoon into prepared muffin pan. Bake for 15–20 minutes or until cooked (when a skewer inserted comes out clean).
3 To make lemon sugar, mix zest, juice and sugar together and drizzle over cakes as soon as they are removed from the oven; the lemon sugar will soak in and set to form a crunchy crust.
4 Allow to cool for 10 minutes before removing from cake tins.

Makes 12

raspberry chocolate friands

The friand (pronounced free-ond) is a little wonder cake that we've all taken to our hearts (and bellies!). I have more than a sneaking suspicion that the term 'friand' is a misnomer, but these sweet treats sure taste good by any name.

100g butter

100g dark cooking chocolate

1 cup ground almonds

1$^1/_2$ cups icing sugar, sifted to remove lumps

$^1/_2$ cup plain flour

1 tablespoon Dutch process cocoa powder

6 egg whites

1 cup raspberries (fresh or unthawed frozen)

icing sugar to dust

1 Heat oven to 180°C on fan-bake. Grease a 12-hole, $^3/_4$-cup capacity, heart-shaped or standard muffin pan. Gently melt butter and chocolate together in a small saucepan, then set aside to cool slightly.

2 Place ground almonds in a mixing bowl and sift over icing sugar, flour and cocoa. Make a well in the centre of these ingredients. Place the melted butter and chocolate and the egg whites (which do not need to be beaten) in the well and stir until just combined. Pour mixture into muffin pans (they should be about $^1/_2$ full), and top each friand with several raspberries. Bake for 25–30 minutes.

3 Allow to stand in pans for 5 minutes before turning out onto a wire rack to cool. Dust with icing sugar to serve.

Makes 12

+ coffee speak ... a long black espresso is a double shot of espresso extracted to 60mls and topped up with boiling water.

+ coffee speak … my favourite coffee is a flat white. This is an antipodean invention and is like a small *caffe latte* served in a cappuccino cup or glass. Usually a flat white is made with a double shot of espresso topped up with steamed milk that is smooth, velvety and therefore 'flat' rather than frothy.

4 things to do with brioche dough

plain brioches

Brioches are divinely buttery and almost cakey-textured breads. Try brioches toasted and slathered with a good fruity jam.

1/4 cup warm water

2 teaspoons active dried yeast

2 tablespoons sugar

4 cups plain flour

1 teaspoon salt

1 cup milk, warmed

2 large eggs, lightly beaten

2 egg yolks

150g butter, softened

1 egg, lightly beaten with a pinch of salt, to glaze

1 Place warm water in a small bowl and sprinkle with yeast and sugar, then leave to activate for about 5 minutes. Once activated, the mixture will foam.

2 Combine flour and salt in a large bowl. Add activated yeast mix, milk, eggs, yolks and softened butter and mix to combine. Turn out onto a lightly floured work surface and knead until smooth and glossy.

3 Place dough in a lightly oiled bowl and cover with plastic wrap. Set in a warm place to rise until doubled in volume; this takes about 1 hour. Knock back dough with your fist and knead slightly.

4 Shape dough into 12 even-sized portions. Place in oiled brioche moulds or mini loaf tins and set aside to rise for 20 minutes. Preheat oven to 190°C.

5 Glaze brioche with beaten egg and bake for 15–20 minutes or until golden brown and firm.

Makes 12

brioches with chocolate centres

Can you believe it – chocolate centres make brioches even more decadent!

1 quantity brioche dough (see opposite)

200g quality dark chocolate, roughly chopped

1 egg, lightly beaten with a pinch of salt, to glaze

1/4 cup granulated white sugar or raw sugar

1 Complete brioche dough to the end of step 3.

2 Shape dough into 12 even-sized portions and press some pieces of chocolate into the centre of each, bringing the dough together to hide the filling. Place seam-side down in oiled brioche moulds and set aside to rise for 20 minutes. Preheat oven to 190°C.

3 Glaze brioche with beaten egg and sprinkle with a little sugar. Bake for 15–20 minutes or until golden brown and firm.

Makes 12

+ coffee ... stimulates digestion, encourages mental activity and lifts the spirits!

blueberry swirl buns

The blueberries melt into the brown sugar
to become jam-like and cling to the spirals of
these buns.

1 quantity brioche dough (see opposite page)

1/2 cup soft brown sugar

1 cup blueberries (fresh or frozen)

1 egg, lightly beaten with a pinch of salt, to glaze

icing sugar to dust

1 Complete brioche dough to the end of step 3.
2 With a rolling pin on a lightly floured work surface, roll out
dough into a 25 x 40cm rectangle. Sprinkle surface with
brown sugar and blueberries and roll up into a log. Cut log
in 4cm portions and place spiral-side upward in lightly oiled,
large-sized muffin pans and set aside to rise for 20 minutes.
Preheat oven to 190°C.
3 Glaze brioche with beaten egg and bake for 15–20
minutes or until golden brown and firm. Dust with icing
sugar to serve.

Makes 10

red pesto spiral loaf

Any pesto, spread or tapenade can be used to
flavour this great savoury snack. Try adding a
scattering of crumbled feta, grated Parmesan or
Cheddar cheese as well.

1 quantity brioche dough (see opposite page)

1 quantity red pesto (see page 22)

1 egg, lightly beaten with a pinch of salt to glaze

sea salt flakes and freshly ground black pepper

1 Complete brioche dough to the end of step 3.
2 With a rolling pin on a lightly floured work surface, roll
out dough into a 25 x 40cm rectangle. Spread surface
with red pesto and roll up into a log. Place on a lightly
oiled oven tray. Set aside to rise for 20 minutes. Preheat
oven to 190°C.
3 Glaze surface of log with beaten egg and sprinkle with
salt flakes and ground pepper. Bake for 15–20 minutes
or until golden brown and firm. Cut slices on an angle
to serve.

Makes 1 loaf

+ coffee speak ... try a
cappuccino with your brioche.
A cappuccino is made with
a single shot of espresso
topped with foamy milk
and sometimes dusted with
a little chocolate powder or
cinnamon.

paprika and parmesan buttermilk scones

Good scones are a wonderful tradition that I learnt from my darling mother, Loraine. These scones are made exceptional by the addition of Parmesan cheese and Spanish smoked paprika.

3 cups self-raising flour

pinch salt

50g butter, cubed

2 teaspoons sweet Spanish smoked paprika

1/2 cup freshly grated Parmesan cheese

1/4 cup chopped fresh parsley or basil

1 1/4 cups buttermilk

extra flour for dusting

1 Preheat oven to 200°C. Place flour and salt in a bowl. Rub butter into flour with fingertips until it resembles breadcrumbs. Stir in paprika, Parmesan and herbs, and make a well in the centre.

2 Pour buttermilk into the well and mix quickly to just combine. Knead mixture very lightly to bring together into a soft dough.

3 Roll out dough to 3cm thick on a board dusted with flour. Cut out rounds with a pastry cutter, or cut into squares if preferred, and place on a greased oven tray.

4 Bake for 10 minutes or until golden brown.

Makes 12

+ substitute ... buttermilk is a cultured milk product with a slightly sour flavour that gives a lighter result to baked goods. Soured milk makes a good substitute if you're unable to find buttermilk in your local supermarket. Add 1 tablespoonful of lemon juice or vinegar to 1 cup of milk (milk must be at room temperature) and leave to stand for 5 minutes to curdle. Use this soured milk in place of buttermilk in any recipe as required.

mushroom and pesto muffins

Mushrooms may sound like a weird flavouring for muffins but I can assure you, these muffins are sensational. Dark field mushrooms are a must as they add all their dramatic depth of colour and flavour.

2 cups self-raising flour, sifted

4 large field mushrooms, very finely chopped

sea salt and freshly ground black pepper

2 tablespoons basil pesto

2 eggs, lightly beaten

1/4 cup olive oil

1 1/2 cups milk

1 Preheat oven to 190°C. Grease a 12-hole, standard muffin pan with butter, or spray with oil.

2 Combine flour and mushrooms in a large bowl and season with salt and pepper. Gently stir in pesto, eggs, oil and milk to just combine. Do not over-mix or the muffins will turn out tough. Spoon into prepared muffin pan.

3 Bake for 25–30 minutes until golden brown and cooked through when tested with a skewer. Remove to a wire rack immediately to prevent sweating.

Makes 12

+ shortcut ... quality store-bought basil pesto is a quick and easy condiment to have on hand in the refrigerator. Add pesto to muffins, salad dressings, soups, stews or whenever a dish needs an extra herbal flavour-boost.

chorizo and rocket bites

Make these more-ish savoury snacks in mini muffin pans – you'll find they're a favourite with everyone, young and old. They freeze well too, and are good to simply reheat straight from frozen when unexpected guests drop in.

2 cups self-raising flour

1 teaspoon baking powder

1/4 teaspoon chilli powder

1/2 cup grated Parmesan cheese

2 chorizo sausages, roughly chopped

1/2 cup roughly chopped rocket leaves

1 medium onion, peeled and finely diced

sea salt and freshly ground black pepper

1 egg, beaten

1/4 cup olive oil

1 3/4 cups milk

1 Preheat oven to 190°C. Spray a 24-hole, mini muffin pan or 12-hole, standard muffin pan with oil, or grease with butter.

2 Sift flour and baking powder into a large bowl. Add chilli, Parmesan, chorizo, rocket, onion, and salt and pepper. Make a well in the centre and pour in egg, oil and milk and stir with a spoon to combine to a smooth batter. Do not over-stir the batter or the muffins will turn out tough.

3 Spoon mixture into prepared tins to just over 3/4 full. Bake mini muffins for 20 minutes and standard muffins for 35 minutes or until firm and golden brown.

Makes 12—24

simple yeast dough

I find this dough very easy to work with and wonderfully versatile. It can be used as a tart base that does not need to be pre-baked, or stuffed with a filling and cooked as calzone, or rolled into mini loaves.

1 teaspoon active dried yeast

1/2 teaspoon sugar

1/4 cup warm water

1 1/2 cups high-grade (strong) flour

1/4 teaspoon salt

1 large egg, at room temperature

50ml olive oil

extra flour for kneading

1 To make the dough, sprinkle yeast and then sugar over warm water in a small bowl and set aside in a warm place to activate for 5–10 minutes (when activated the mixture will be frothy).

2 Place flour and salt in a large bowl and make a well in the centre. Break egg into the well with the oil and pour in the frothy yeast mixture. Mix with a wooden spoon and bring together to form a soft dough. Place dough in a lightly oiled bowl, cover with cling film and leave to rise for 45 minutes, or until doubled in size.

3 Punch back dough with the fist of your hand. Knead briefly before using in desired recipe.

Makes enough dough for a 20cm tart or 4-6 stuffed loaves or small tarts

cheese and vegetable loaves

These loaves also work well as transportable and tasty picnic food.

1 recipe simple yeast dough (see opposite)

filling

3 tablespoons olive oil

1 onion, peeled and chopped

1 cup small broccoli florets

1 red pepper, seeds removed and sliced

1/4 cup pine nuts

1/4 cup fruit chutney of choice

100g blue cheese or goats' cheese

1 Heat a wok or frying pan and stir-fry vegetables and pine nuts in oil for 5 minutes or until the vegatables are tender. Set aside to cool.

2 Spray 6 mini loaf tins or large muffin tins with olive oil. Cut dough into 6 equal portions. On a lightly floured work surface flatten each piece of dough into a circle. Divide cold vegetable filling by 6 and place a portion in the centre of each disc of dough. Top with a teaspoon of chutney and some cheese. Bring the edges of the dough together to cover filling. Place each bundle into prepared tins. Leave to rise in a warm place for 30 minutes.

3 Preheat oven to 200°C. Bake loaves for 15–20 minutes or until golden brown and firm.

Makes 6

+ my advice … use the appropriate flour for each specific purpose. Use 'high-grade' flour or 'strong' flour for bread dough as these flours contain more gluten (protein) and are specially formulated for bread-making. Use 'standard' or 'plain' flour for making cakes and biscuits as this is formulated to produce soft-textured baked items. Tipo 00 flour is light and fragrant and a good quality, all-purpose flour.

spanish tartlets

In the Basque region of Spain, morsels of this type are called pintxos; Basque bars are dedicated to serving grand counter-top displays of such snacks.

1 measure savoury shortcrust pastry (see page 87)
2 cups cherry tomatoes, halved
2 roast red peppers (see page 23) sliced or 225g jar sliced piquillo pimientos
1/2 cup torn fresh basil leaves
2 cloves garlic, crushed
1/2 teaspoon sweet Spanish smoked paprika
sea salt and freshly ground black pepper
3 tablespoons extra virgin olive oil
100g soft goats' cheese, coarsely crumbled

1 Roll out pastry to 3mm thick and use to line 12 8cm brioche or tartlet moulds. Prick bases with a fork and chill for 30 minutes. Preheat oven to 200°C.
2 Line the pastry cases with foil and fill with baking beans and place in oven to blind-bake for 10 minutes. Remove foil and beans and return pastry cases to the oven for a further 5 minutes. Remove to a wire rack to cool.
3 Combine halved cherry tomatoes, red peppers, basil and garlic in a bowl. Sprinkle with paprika and season with salt and pepper to taste. Drizzle with olive oil and toss well.
4 Arrange mounds of vegetable mixture and coarsely crumbled goats' cheese in pastry cases to serve.

Makes 12

tomato and caper tarts

Biting into these tarts causes the topping tomatoes to burst and spill their concentrated flavour over the soft bread base.

1 recipe simple yeast dough (see page 68)
2 cups cherry tomatoes
1/2 cup capers, drained
olive oil
sea salt and freshly ground black pepper

1 Heat oven to 190°C. Lightly oil a baking tray.
2 Divide dough into 4 or 6 even pieces. On a lightly floured work surface, flatten each portion of dough into a circle.
3 Divide filling ingredients between dough circles, pressing cherry tomatoes into the surface and scattering with capers. Be sure to leave a 1cm frame free of topping. Drizzle each tart with a little olive oil and season with salt and pepper.
4 Bake tarts for 15–20 minutes until edges are puffed and golden brown.

Makes 4-6

+ my advice ... made in advance and well covered, this simple yeast dough will keep in the fridge for 2 days. Alternatively, it can be frozen for up to 3 months. Bring the dough to room temperature before using it in any chosen recipe.

nonettes

Along with friands and madeleines, nonettes are yet another clever, French sweet creation. They are small, iced, ginger cakes filled with marmalade. For ease, I've included marmalade in the mix.

125g butter

$^1/_2$ cup brown sugar, tightly packed

$^2/_3$ cup milk

$^1/_4$ cup orange marmalade

$^1/_4$ cup golden syrup

1 cup plus 2 tablespoons self-raising flour

1 teaspoon bicarbonate of soda (baking soda)

1 tablespoon ground ginger

1 teaspoon ground cinnamon

$^1/_2$ teaspoon ground nutmeg

1 egg, beaten

1 Preheat oven to 160°C on fan-bake. Grease 12 $^1/_2$-cup capacity, mini cake tins or a 12-hole, standard muffin pan with butter or oil and lightly dust with flour.

2 Place butter, brown sugar, milk, marmalade and golden syrup in a saucepan and gently melt over a medium heat, stirring occasionally. Remove to cool.

3 Place flour, bicarbonate of soda and spices in a bowl and make a well in the centre. Add the egg and cooled liquid to the well and stir to combine into a smooth batter. Spoon mixture into prepared tins to $^3/_4$ full and bake for 30 minutes or until a skewer inserted comes out clean. Remove to a wire rack to cool.

4 Once cold, drizzle nonettes with lemon icing (see opposite for method).

Makes 12

+ how to ... make lemon icing: in a bowl combine 1 1/2 cups icing sugar (sifted to remove lumps) with the juice of 1 lemon and 1–2 tablespoons boiling water, and stir until smooth and of a pourable consistency. Using boiling water helps the icing to set with a glass-like finish as it cools.

vanilla sugar madeleines

Madeleines are high on the hit-list of the best little cake creations ever invented. They are traditionally cooked in scallop shell-shaped tins. A mere madeleine famously swept Marcel Proust away with 'an exquisite pleasure' – proving that once tried, madeleines will not be forgotten.

½ cup (70g packet) blanched almonds

1 cup icing sugar

2 large eggs

2 egg whites

⅓ cup vanilla caster sugar (see below)

1 teaspoon vanilla extract

¾ cup plain flour

pinch salt

100g butter, melted and cooled

vanilla icing sugar to dust

1 Place almonds and icing sugar in the bowl of a food processor and grind until very fine. In another bowl whisk eggs, egg whites, vanilla caster sugar and vanilla extract together to combine. Sift flour and salt and fold with almond mixture into egg mixture to form a batter.

2 Fold melted butter into batter; the mixture will be quite runny. Cover and chill for 2–24 hours so that the mixture thickens.

3 When ready to cook madeleines, preheat oven to 190°C. Spray madeleine shell moulds with oil and place 1 tablespoon of mixture in each. Bake for 10 minutes until puffed in the centre, firm and golden. Remove to a wire rack to cool. Repeat with remaining batter.

4 Dust with vanilla icing sugar to serve. Madelines will last for up to 4 days stored in an airtight container.

Makes 24

ginger-beer fruit loaf

I will always have a soft spot for fruit loaf. When I was a child, I baked many a fruit loaf for my grandmother, Alice, as this was her favourite special treat.

200g dried apricots

200g raisins

250g sultanas

½ teaspoon bicarbonate of soda (baking soda)

1½ cups ginger-beer

½ cup golden syrup

2 large eggs, lightly beaten

½ cup brown sugar, tightly packed

1¼ cups self-raising flour

pinch salt

2 teaspoons ground cinnamon

1 teaspoon mixed spice

1 Place dried fruit in a bowl and sprinkle with bicarbonate of soda. Heat ginger-beer and golden syrup in a saucepan and pour over fruit. Cover with plastic wrap and leave to soak overnight.

2 Next day, preheat oven to 160°C on fan-bake. Grease and flour an 11 x 25 x 7cm loaf tin.

3 Stir beaten eggs and brown sugar into soaked fruit. Sift in flour, salt and spices and stir to combine. Spoon mixture into prepared tin. Bake for 1 hour or until a skewer inserted comes out clean. Remove to a wire rack to cool.

4 Serve sliced and spread with butter if desired. This fruit loaf will last for up to 5 days if stored in an airtight container.

Makes 1 loaf

+ my advice ... there are two ways to create vanilla sugar: one is to place whole vanilla beans in stored sugar (this can be icing, caster, white or raw sugar) and the sugar will take on the gentle fragrance and taste of vanilla; a second way is to process roughly chopped vanilla beans in a food processor with the sugar to be flavoured. This sugar then needs to be sifted to remove the excess bits of vanilla bean but results in a much stronger vanilla flavour, plus leaves lots of pretty black vanilla speckles in the sugar.

+ coffee speak ... *a caffe latte* is made with a double shot of espresso topped up with velvety, steamed milk. I like mine served in a glass.

04.po:

Take time out on a warm and carefree day. Pack transportable make-ahead treats. Go day tripping, boating, to the beach, or visit a tranquil garden.

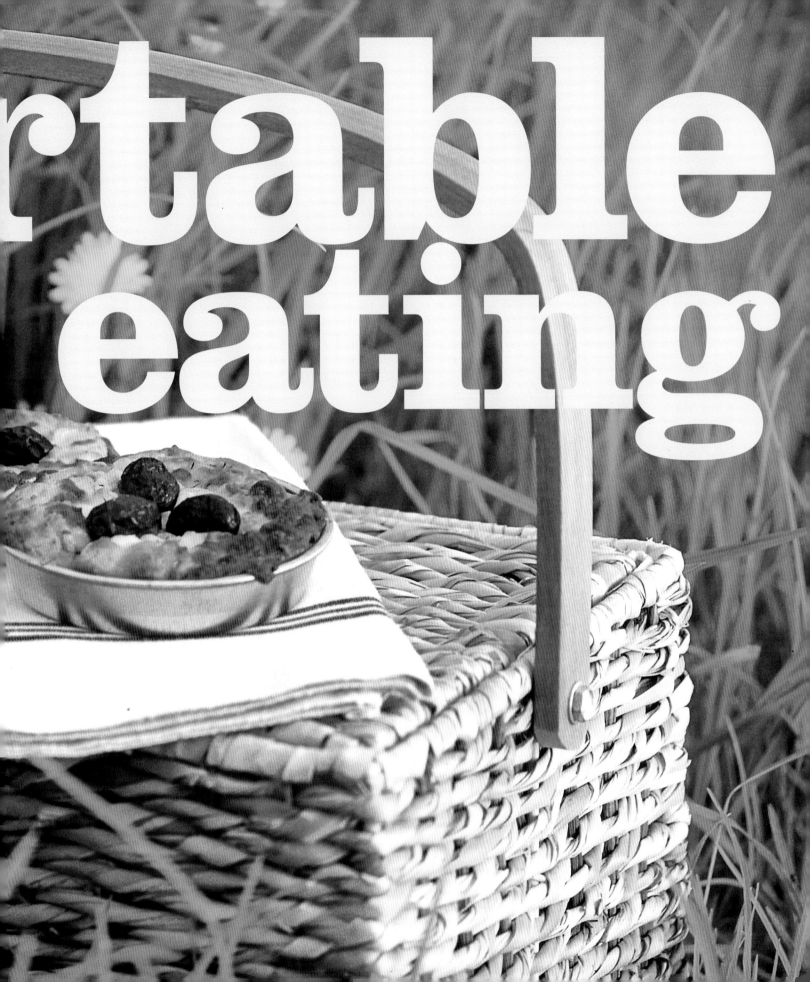

lamb, olive and rosemary mini meat loaves

These mini meat loaves are jam-packed full of flavour and are therefore designed to be eaten cold.

1kg lamb mince

1 red onion, peeled and chopped

4 cloves garlic, peeled and chopped

2 tablespoons olive oil

1/2 cup fresh breadcrumbs

1 egg, lightly beaten

sea salt and freshly ground black pepper

1/2 cup stuffed green olives

1 tablespoon chopped fresh rosemary

juice and zest of 2 lemons

8 slices rindless bacon

1 Preheat oven to 200°C. Lightly oil 8 individual loaf pans or 8 large muffin pans.
2 Combine all ingredients (except bacon) in a bowl and mix until well blended. Divide mixture into 8 equal portions and mould to fit the shape of chosen pans. Wrap each loaf in a slice of bacon and place one in each pan. Bake for 20–25 minutes until golden brown.
3 Remove from pans to cool, then refrigerate. Keep cold during transport.

Serves 8

+ serving suggestions ... wrap mini meat loaves in greaseproof paper and serve whole with a pottle of chutney to dollop over or dip in. Pesto is also a great accompaniment. Or slice meat loaves and layer between slices of bread to make tasty sandwiches.

basil and lemon tortilla sandwich

This tortilla could be called a Spanish omelette and can be served as tapas, between bread or elegantly solo. Tortilla is delicious eaten hot or cold so can be prepared the day before if necessary.

4 large eggs

1/4 cup cream or milk

finely grated zest of 1 lemon

sea salt and freshly ground black pepper

2 onions, peeled and sliced

4 tablespoons olive oil

lots of fresh basil leaves

divided flat bread, such as focaccia

1 In a bowl whisk eggs with milk or cream and lemon zest. Season well with salt and pepper.
2 In a 24cm, non-stick frying pan sweat onions in olive oil for 5–10 minutes over a low heat until softened. Raise the heat and pour in the egg mixture. Pull the edges of the mixture away from the sides of the pan towards the centre so that the wet mixture fills the spaces and cooks.
3 When egg is set and base of tortilla is golden brown, invert the tortilla onto a dinner plate. Slip the tortilla back into the pan and cook for a few minutes more to brown the other side.
4 Sandwich fresh basil leaves and the tortilla between divided flat bread. Cut into 4 portions.

Serves 4

+ serving suggestion ... better still, moisten the bread with the juice of a gently squeezed tomato as they do in Catalonia, Spain.

+ my favourite ... a citrus zester is invaluable to create strands of citrus peel in a jiffy. This small tool has a row of little holes for making long thin threads of zest. If you don't have one of these, you can use a vegetable peeler to peel strips of zest from the fruit. Use a sharp knife to cut these strips into fine strands.

tomato, bocconcini and basil mini-loaf sandwiches

Tasty sandwiches are easy to transport and always popular.

6 mini brioches (see page 62) or small bread rolls

1/4 cup green pesto (see page 22)

6 bocconcini (baby balls of mozzarella), sliced

6 small ripe tomatoes, sliced and drained on paper towels

sea salt and freshly ground black pepper

1/2 cup fresh basil leaves

1 Slice the mini brioche loaves or bread rolls into 6 slices. Spread a little pesto on one side of each slice.
2 Make 3 mini sandwiches from each loaf by topping 3 slices of bread with a few slices of bocconcini and tomato, salt and pepper and a basil leaf or two. Top with remaining slices of bread and reform into a loaf.
3 Repeat with each brioche or roll. Wrap in greaseproof paper.

Makes 6

+ substitute ... if sometimes you don't have time to make your own brioche loaves, any small bread roll would be suitable.

spiced chicken and mint salad wrap

Fill and transport these wraps close to the time you will be eating them. Otherwise, to prevent soggy wraps, pack the filling ingredients in covered containers for transportation. On arrival, lay the flat breads on clean tea towels, spread with filling and wrap as you go.

2 skinless chicken breasts, finely sliced

2 tablespoons yoghurt

1 teaspoon each ground coriander, paprika, cumin

sea salt and freshly ground black pepper

olive oil

4 thin, flat, Lebanese naan breads, pita or tortilla wraps

1 cup baby spinach leaves

1 avocado, stone removed, peeled and sliced

2 tablespoons chopped fresh mint leaves

1 Combine chicken, yoghurt and spices in a bowl and season with salt and pepper. Toss well to coat chicken in spice mixture. Heat a frying pan, add a little oil and cook chicken in 2–3 batches, tossing regularly for 4–5 minutes until browned all over. Refrigerate chicken to cool.
2 Lay chosen flat breads on a work surface. Cover each with a few spinach leaves, sliced avocado, chopped fresh mint and cold chicken. Season with salt and pepper and roll up to enclose filling.

Serves 4

+ my advice ... buy dried spices in small amounts. As they lose their potency with age, write the date of purchase on packets of spices so that you know how old they are and when to throw them out. Keep for no longer than 6 months. Preferably grind your own powder from whole spices and lightly toast spices to heighten flavours before incorporating in dishes.

+ my advice ... process leftover bread into fresh breadcrumbs and freeze in zip-lock plastic bags for later use. They will defrost in a jiffy.

asparagus and red pesto chicken rolls

I often serve this dish when I'm entertaining. It's great served hot for lunch or dinner parties, but also works well served cold as fun food-to-go.

6 skinless chicken breasts
6 slices of bacon, rinds removed

red pesto stuffing

1 cup red pesto (see page 22)
1 cup fresh white breadcrumbs
sea salt and freshly ground black pepper
12 fresh asparagus spears

1 Preheat oven to 190°C. Place chicken breasts on a work surface with what was the skin-side down. Pound chicken breasts with a meat mallet to flatten a little.
2 Place red pesto and breadcrumbs in a bowl and mix to combine. Spread this stuffing over the surface of each chicken breast. Season with salt and pepper. Place 2 spears of asparagus lengthways on chicken and roll chicken up around asparagus to form a log shape. Wrap a slice of bacon around each chicken breast roll to secure and place in an oven pan.
3 Roast for 20 minutes, then remove to rest for 10 minutes before slicing in half or into 2cm thick medallions.

Serves 6

... good idea ... disposable noodle boxes, chopsticks and cutlery are compact to pack and make light work of cleaning up after a movable feast.

tomato and parmesan rice cakes

feta and olive pies

tomato and parmesan rice cakes

These rice cakes are wonderfully soft and light and make a great base for any flavouring. Try adding grated courgette, sweetcorn kernels, chopped mushrooms or blue cheese for a change.

1 cup long-grain, basmati or Jasmine rice

oil to grease pan

1/4 cup dried breadcrumbs to dust pans

400g can chopped tomatoes

3 spring onions, finely sliced

1/2 cup milk

6 eggs, lightly beaten

1/2 cup grated fresh Parmesan cheese

1/2 cup grated Cheddar cheese

1/4 cup chopped fresh basil

sea salt and freshly ground black pepper

3 medium tomatoes, thinly sliced

1 Cook rice in plenty of boiling salted water for 12 minutes. Drain well and transfer to a bowl to cool.

2 Preheat oven to 180°C. Grease and dust with breadcrumbs 12 individual, 3/4-cup capacity, round- or square-shaped muffin pans.

3 Mix remaining ingredients, except sliced tomato, with cold rice and season well with salt and pepper. Spoon mixture into prepared pans and place a slice of tomato on top of each. Bake for 35–45 minutes or until a skewer inserted in the centre comes out clean.

4 Serve hot or cold with a favourite chutney if desired. These rice cakes will last 2–3 days if stored in the fridge. They can also be frozen if necessary – warm after thawing to serve.

Makes 12

+ my advice ... save rinds of Parmesan for flavouring other dishes; wrap them in plastic wrap and freeze. They can be added to hearty stocks, soups and stews, or used to enrich any dish with a rich, piquant, cheesy taste.

feta and olive pies

These pies are incredibly simple and meltingly delicious.

3 onions, sliced

1/4 cup olive oil

1 cup self-raising flour

3 large eggs, lightly beaten

1 cup thick plain yoghurt

300g feta cheese, cubed

1 cup freshly grated Gruyère cheese

3 tablespoons chopped fresh dill

sea salt and freshly ground black pepper

1/2 cup Kalamata olives

1 Cook onions in oil for 10 minutes to soften but not brown. Remove to one side. Preheat oven to 180°C. Grease 8 10cm pie tins.

2 Place flour in a bowl and make a well in the centre. Add eggs and yoghurt in the well, then stir with a wooden spoon to combine. Stir in cooled onions, feta, Gruyère and dill. Season with salt and pepper.

3 Pour mixture into prepared tins, level surface and place a few olives on each. Bake individual pies for 25 minutes or until golden and set.

4 Cool a little before removing from tins.

Serves 8

+ good idea ... to protect pies during transport, pack them in the tins in which they are cooked.

bacon, egg and pea pies

Classic and irresistible picnic food with a modern twist.

300g savoury shortcrust or puff pastry (see opposite)

250g rindless bacon

2 tablespoons chopped fresh parsley

6 large eggs

sea salt and freshly ground black pepper

2 cups thawed frozen peas or blanched fresh garden peas

1 Roll out pastry to 3mm thick and use to line 4 deep-sided, 1½-cup capacity cake tins. Prick pastry bases and chill well. Preheat oven to 200°C.

2 Line pastry bases with bacon and parsley, and break one egg into each. Break remaining 2 eggs into a bowl, beat lightly and season with salt and pepper. Scatter surface of each pie with ½ cup of peas and top with a little of the beaten egg divided between the 4 pies.

3 Bake individual pies for 15 minutes, then loosely cover with foil to prevent tops becoming too dark. Reduce temperature to 170°C and bake for a further 15 minutes or until filling is firm and pastry is golden brown.

Serves 4

+ how to make ... savoury shortcrust pastry: place 225g plain flour and a pinch of salt in a bowl. Use your fingertips to rub 180g cubed cold butter into the flour (or use a food processor to process), until the mix resembles fine breadcrumbs.

Stir in 3–4 tablespoons ice-cold water with a knife, adding just enough water to form a firm dough. Turn dough out on a floured work surface and knead lightly until smooth.

Wrap dough in plastic wrap and chill for 20–30 minutes before use.

sesame greens in a noodle box

Any seasonal greens are enhanced by the addition of sesame oil and seeds.

250g asparagus, trimmed

250g snow peas, trimmed

250g green beans, trimmed

2 tablespoons sesame oil

sea salt and freshly ground black pepper

2 teaspoons each, toasted black and white sesame seeds

1 Blanch green vegetables in boiling salted water for 1–2 minutes or until just tender. Drain well and plunge into ice-cold water to cool and to retain their bright green colour. Once cold, drain well.

2 Toss with sesame oil and season to taste with salt and pepper. Sprinkle with sesame seeds to serve.

Serves 2

peanut noodle box salad

Adults and children alike adore this crunchy peanut noodle salad.

250g egg noodles

peanut dressing

1 cup crunchy peanut butter

3 tablespoons grated fresh ginger

3 cloves garlic, peeled and crushed

3 tablespoons Thai sweet chilli sauce

$1/2$ cup light soy sauce

$1/2$ cup roughly chopped fresh coriander leaves

1 Cook noodles in boiling salted water for 2–3 minutes, or according to packet instructions, until just tender. Drain and refresh with cold water. Drain well again, then set aside.

2 To make the dressing, place peanut butter, ginger, garlic, chilli and soy sauces in a bowl and stir to combine.

3 Toss noodles with peanut dressing to coat. Serve topped with chopped fresh coriander if desired.

Serves 4

+ my advice ... cook the noodles and make the dressing ahead, then toss these together as and when you need to. The dressing will last for up to 4 days if stored covered in the refrigerator.

+ noodle boxes also make great containers for packaging edible gifts. For instance, fill them with hand-made cookies, tie with pretty ribbons and delight your friends.

smoky roast red pepper soup in a flask

In summer I like to serve this soup chilled, with a few ice cubes floating on the surface.

4 red peppers, stalks and seeds removed

olive oil

1 red onion, peeled and sliced

2 cloves garlic, peeled and crushed

1 litre tomato juice

1 tablespoon raw sugar

2 teaspoons sweet Spanish smoked paprika

2 tablespoons finely chopped fresh basil

sea salt and freshly ground black pepper

1 Preheat oven to 190°C. Place peppers in a roasting pan, drizzle with olive oil and roast for 30 minutes, tossing occasionally, until soft and the skin is blistered. Remove to a bowl, cover with plastic wrap and leave to cool. Once cold the skins can easily be slipped off.

2 At the same time, heat a saucepan with ¼ cup olive oil and cook onion and garlic over a gentle heat for 10 minutes until softened but not coloured. Add tomato juice and sugar and simmer for 5 minutes. Add paprika, basil and season with salt and pepper.

3 Purée cold pepper and tomato mixture in a blender until smooth; this will need to be done in 2–3 batches. Check and adjust seasoning if necessary. Reheat to piping hot, pour into a flask to transport and serve with crusty bread. Or serve chilled, stored in a flask to maintain its temperature.

Serves 4-6

+ my favourite spice … is La Chinata Spanish smoked paprika. This versatile spice has many possibilities. For starters, try adding smoked paprika to creamy mashed potato; or to tomato, pumpkin or carrot soup; sprinkle some over roasted vegetables or whisk a teaspoonful into a vinaigrette.

jerusalem artichoke soup in a flask

When Jerusalem artichokes are in season, I recommend making this soup regularly, or at least enough to make the taste memory last until next year's crop!

1 tablespoon olive oil

25g butter

2 onions, chopped

2 cloves garlic, chopped

500g Jerusalem artichokes, scrubbed and roughly chopped

300g potatoes, peeled and chopped

1 litre chicken or vegetable stock

sea salt and freshly ground white pepper

1/4 cup cream

1 In a saucepan heat oil and butter to melt, add onions and garlic and cook over a gentle heat for 10–15 minutes to soften but not colour. Add artichokes, potatoes and stock, and bring to the boil. Simmer for 30 minutes until vegetables are tender.

2 Cool a little before liquidising in a blender. Leave chunky if desired, or for a smooth soup strain through a sieve to remove texture. Season to taste with salt and pepper.

3 Add cream and gently reheat to serve. Pour into a flask and seal to transport.

Serves 4-6

+ serving suggestion ... pack a pottle of pesto in a hamper with the soup flask. Serve mugs of soup with a dollop of pesto on top so that the tastes and textures meld as you sip.

extra-thick ginger crunch

I have developed an extra-thick version of
ginger crunch that is even more compelling
than the original of my childhood memories.
If you love the flavour of ginger, then this is
just for you!

1½ cups plain flour

1 teaspoon baking powder

1 teaspoon ground ginger

½ cup caster sugar

125g butter, cubed

topping

150g butter

¼ cup golden syrup

2 cups icing sugar, sifted to remove lumps

1 tablespoon ground ginger

¼ cup roughly chopped crystallized ginger

1 Preheat oven to 180°C. Line a 17 x 27cm, deep-sided
slice tin with non-stick baking paper to come up the sides
of the tin.

2 Place flour, baking powder, ginger and sugar in the
bowl of a food processor and pulse to sift. Add butter and
process to resemble fine breadcrumbs or rub in butter by
hand. Press crumbs evenly over base of prepared tin.
Bake for 25 minutes until golden brown.

3 To make topping, place butter and golden syrup in a
saucepan to melt over a medium heat. Add icing sugar
and ground ginger and cook for 1 minute, stirring constantly
to combine until smooth. Stir in crystallized ginger.

4 Pour topping over base and leave to cool and set.
Remove from tin and cut into bars or squares to serve.
Ginger crunch will last for up to 5 days stored in an
airtight container.

Makes 18

+ good idea ... make a sheet of slice on
the weekend, cut it into squares and
store in an airtight container. This way
you have treats to pop into mid-week
lunch-boxes.

caramel walnut square

Slices are such a good invention and are
perfectly built for transportation. Pack a few
more pieces than you need, as one per person
is never enough!

180g butter

½ cup sugar

1 teaspoon vanilla extract

1 cup plain flour

½ cup wholemeal flour

1 teaspoon baking powder

topping

100g butter

¼ cup golden syrup

395g can sweetened condensed milk

1 cup walnut pieces

1 Preheat oven to 180°C. Line a 17 x 27cm, deep-sided
slice tin with non-stick baking paper to come up the sides
of the tin.

2 In a bowl beat butter, sugar and vanilla until creamy. Stir
in flours and baking powder. Reserve ¼ cup of this mix
and spread remaining mix into the base of the prepared tin.

3 To make the topping, melt butter, golden syrup and
condensed milk in a saucepan. Bring to the boil then
simmer for 3–5 minutes, stirring constantly to slightly
caramelise the mixture. Pour caramel over prepared base.
Scatter with walnut pieces and crumbled reserved base
mixture.

4 Bake for 30–40 minutes or until golden and filling is set.
Cool, remove from tin and cut into bars or squares to serve.

Makes 18

+ substitute ... any other nut for the
walnuts in this recipe if you prefer. Try
pecans, macadamias, hazelnuts or Brazil
nuts for a change.

05.sa

lads
to share

Mixed sensory delights of tastes and texture bring pleasure to the palate. Salads are the perfect spontaneous meal. Great food to share with family and friends.

+ how to ... toast nuts or seeds. Place the nuts or seeds in a small oven pan, or frying pan with an ovenproof handle, and roast at 180°C for 10–20 minutes, depending on size of seed or nut, or until golden brown. Watch carefully as they can burn quickly, and shake or stir once or twice during cooking.

roasted vegetable salad with hazelnut dressing

Any combination of vegetables suitable for roasting can be used in this salad. Try substituting or adding sliced pumpkin, parsnips or quartered red onions for a change.

500g baby carrots, scrubbed and trimmed
250g baby beetroots, scrubbed and trimmed
250g baby fennel bulbs, trimmed and halved
olive oil
sea salt and freshly ground black pepper
½ cup toasted hazelnuts

hazelnut dressing

1 tablespoon seed mustard
3 tablespoons balsamic vinegar
¼ cup hazelnut oil or extra virgin olive oil
sea salt and freshly ground black pepper

1 Preheat oven to 200°C. Toss all prepared vegetables in a little olive oil and season with salt and pepper. Place vegetables in an oven pan and roast for 25–35 minutes until golden brown, tossing once during cooking. It may pay to roast beetroot separately as it can bleed and discolour the other vegetables. Remove vegetables to cool.
2 In a small bowl whisk mustard, balsamic vinegar and oil together to form a dressing. Season to taste with salt and pepper.
3 Toss vegetables in dressing and serve scattered with toasted hazelnuts.

Serves 4

roasted asparagus salad with broad beans, almonds and bacon

Roasting asparagus is a wonderful way to prepare this green vegetable as the spears caramelise and gain a nice, almost nutty, taste.

500g fresh asparagus

extra virgin olive oil

2 cloves garlic, crushed

sea salt

4 slices rindless bacon

200g broad beans, shelled (see page 107 for details)

1/4 cup slivered almonds, toasted

2–3 tablespoons torn fresh basil leaves

freshly ground black pepper

1 Preheat oven to 200°C. Snap woody ends from asparagus spears and spread out on an oven tray. Drizzle with a little olive oil and scatter with crushed garlic, then rub asparagus to evenly coat with oil. Sprinkle asparagus with salt and roast for 10 minutes or until golden brown, tossing once during cooking. Remove to a serving platter to cool.

2 Grill bacon until crispy, drain and cool on paper towels, then cut or break into pieces. Peel the skins off the broad beans to reveal the bright green beans within.

3 To serve, scatter bacon pieces, broad beans, toasted almonds, basil and a grinding of black pepper over the platter of cold asparagus.

Serves 4

angel-hair salad

This gloriously delicate pasta salad can be served many ways; either as a light meal in itself or as a side to a simple main, such as barbecued or pan-fried fish, meat or chicken.

250g angel-hair pasta or tagliolini

1/2 cup extra virgin olive oil

2 cloves garlic, crushed

2 cups cherry tomatoes, halved

1 small red chilli, seeds removed and finely chopped

2 roast red peppers (see page 23) sliced, or 225g jar sliced piquillo pimientos

3 tablespoons white wine vinegar

sea salt and freshly ground black pepper

1/3 cup slivered or chopped pistachio nuts

1 Cook pasta in plenty of boiling salted water for 2–3 minutes or according to packet instructions, until al dente. Drain well, toss with oil and garlic and set aside to cool.

2 Combine cold pasta with cherry tomatoes, chilli, peppers and vinegar and toss well. Season with salt and pepper to taste and serve scattered with pistachio nuts.

Serves 4-6

+ visual impact ... use unexpected vessels to present food in a different way. For instance, use coffee cups and saucers or glasses as containers for soup or individual servings of salads or desserts.

prawn salad with preserved lemon dressing

Recipe instructions will often say that prawns need to be de-veined. You can do this easily by running the tip of a sharp knife down the back of the prawns and lifting out the dark veins.

500g raw prawns, peeled with tails intact, de-veined

1 telegraph cucumber

1 bunch watercress, leaves removed from stems

1 bulb fennel, trimmed and finely sliced

150g feta cheese, crumbled

1 preserved lemon (see note opposite)

preserved lemon dressing

1 tablespoon preserved lemon liquid

3 tablespoons verjuice (or white wine vinegar)

¼ cup extra virgin olive oil

freshly ground black pepper

1 Heat a saucepan with 3cm water in the base. Place prawns in the water to gently poach for 1–2 minutes, turning prawns if necessary until they turn bright pink. Remove to a plate and refrigerate to cool.

2 Cut cucumber in half lengthways and remove seeds by running a teaspoon down the centre of the cucumber. Roughly dice cucumber flesh and place in a large bowl with watercress, fennel, feta and cold prawns.

3 Remove flesh from preserved lemon and discard. Finely dice the rind and add to the salad bowl.

4 To make the dressing, in a small bowl combine the preserved lemon liquid with the verjuice and olive oil and season to taste with pepper (the preserved lemon and feta provide a salty taste to this salad). Pour dressing over salad and toss well.

Serves 4

+ how to make ... preserved lemons. Take clean lemons and divide in quarters, not quite cutting all the way through and leaving the base intact. Place plenty of coarse sea or rock salt into the cuts of each lemon. Pack lemons into an appropriately sized, sterilised jar. Add a little more salt, and fill any remaining space with extra lemon juice. Seal jar and store for 1 month before using. Shake the jar every day for the first week. Refrigerate once opened.

+ good idea ... it is advisable to store bottled Thai fish sauce in the refrigerator after opening to protect it from deterioration.

salmon and red cabbage slaw with hot and sour dressing

I think these are the most complementary flavours and textures to team with salmon, plus the freshness of the dressing tones down the richness of this lusciously oily fish.

400g hot-smoked salmon, broken into small pieces

1/2 red cabbage, finely shredded

250g snow peas or green beans, trimmed and finely sliced

1 carrot, peeled and cut into fine strips

1 red pepper, finely sliced, stalks and seeds removed

4 spring onions, trimmed and sliced

1/2 cup chopped fresh coriander leaves

1/2 cup roasted peanuts

hot and sour dressing

3 tablespoons Thai sweet chilli sauce

juice of 2–3 limes, to taste

1 tablespoon light soy sauce

1 tablespoon fish sauce

1 tablespoon sesame oil

1 Place all salad ingredients in a large bowl.
2 Combine dressing ingredients in a small bowl, adding a little more of each ingredient to taste if necessary to gain the perfect blend of hot, sweet, sour and salty components. Pour dressing over salad and toss well.

Serves 4

+ my advice ... frozen broad beans are an excellent product. All you need to do is place them in a bowl and pour boiling water over them. Drain well and peel off the tough outer skin to reveal the vivid green and tender bean within.

4 side salads

red salad

I think that this festive and flavourful bright red salad is a great recipe to make at Christmas time.

1kg red peppers, halved and seeds removed

olive oil

500g medium-sized, ripe tomatoes

½ cup sun-dried tomatoes

red dressing

reserved pepper halves

2 cloves garlic, peeled

2 tablespoons fresh marjoram (or oregano)

3 tablespoons red wine vinegar

3 tablespoons extra virgin olive oil

sea salt and freshly ground black pepper

1 Preheat the oven to 200°C. Place the red pepper halves in an oven pan and drizzle with a little olive oil. Roast for 30 minutes or until the skins blister and the flesh is soft. Remove to a bowl and cover with plastic wrap so that the peppers sweat and the skins loosen. Once cool enough to handle, the skins can easily be pulled off. Reserve 2 halves for the dressing.

2 Roughly slice each pepper half into 4–5 pieces and cut the tomatoes into wedges. Place these ingredients in a salad bowl with the sun-dried tomatoes.

3 To make the dressing, place the reserved red pepper, garlic, marjoram, vinegar and extra virgin olive oil in the bowl of a food processor and process to form a smooth dressing. Season with salt and pepper to taste. Pour dressing over salad ingredients and toss well to serve.

Serves 6 as a side salad

confetti orzo

Orzo pasta has a magical silky texture that contrasts with all these different flavours and textures.

1 cup orzo pasta (rice-shaped pasta)

3 cloves garlic, crushed

¼ cup extra virgin olive oil

½ cup quality black olives, pitted and roughly chopped

1 cup sweetcorn kernels

1 red pepper, seeds removed and finely diced

¼ cup chopped fresh flat leaf parsley

3–4 tablespoons white wine vinegar

sea salt and freshly ground black pepper

1 Cook orzo in plenty of salted, boiling water for about 10 minutes or until al dente (tender to the bite). Drain well. Place in a bowl, toss through garlic and olive oil to prevent pasta sticking together and set aside to cool.

2 Combine remaining ingredients with cold orzo and toss well. Season with salt and pepper to taste.

Serves 6 as a side salad

+ my advice ... cook pasta in plenty of water at a rolling boil so that it does not stick together.

indian spiced carrot salad

When heated, the mustard seeds burst and give
the carrots a special aromatic pungency.

500g carrots, peeled and grated lengthways

1 tablespoon sugar

3 tablespoons white wine vinegar

¼ cup vegetable oil, such as canola,
    sunflower or grapeseed oil

2 tablespoons black mustard seeds

2 teaspoons fennel seeds

sea salt and freshly ground black pepper

¼ cup chopped fresh coriander

1 Place grated carrots in a bowl and sprinkle with sugar
and vinegar. Toss well and set aside.
2 Heat a frying pan, add the oil, mustard and fennel seeds
and cook for about a minute until seeds start to pop.
Remove from the heat and pour immediately over carrots.
3 Toss well and season with salt and pepper to taste.
Serve scattered with fresh coriander.

Serves 6 as a side salad

beetroot, lime and sesame salad

I like to serve this salad with pan-fried, fresh
fish fillets as the flavours work really well
together.

1kg beetroot, scrubbed

¼ cup roughly chopped, fresh mint leaves

lime dressing

juice and finely grated zest of 2 limes

2 tablespoons sesame oil

3 tablespoons toasted sesame seeds

sea salt and freshly ground black pepper

1 Cook whole beetroot in plenty of boiling, salted water
until tender; this may take up to an hour depending on the
size of the beetroot. Drain and set aside to cool, then peel
(the skins will simply slip off). Cut cooked beetroot into
thick strips and place in a salad bowl.
2 Whisk the dressing ingredients to combine and season
with salt and pepper to taste. Pour dressing over beetroot
and toss well. Serve scattered with chopped fresh mint.

Serves 6 as a side salad

+ serving suggestion ... make all 4 side salads and serve as a
mixed salad plate for a light lunch.

tarragon chicken salad

spiced couscous salad with lamb and feta

tarragon chicken salad

Tarragon is a much-underrated herb – here it adds a fresh and aromatic zing to chicken salad.

1 whole corn-fed, free-range chicken

1 bay leaf

1 onion, peeled and quartered

1 carrot, roughly chopped

cold water, to cover

1 cos lettuce

creamy tarragon dressing

1/2 cup light sour cream

2 spring onions, finely sliced

2 stalks celery, finely diced

1/4 cup white wine vinegar

2 tablespoons chopped fresh tarragon leaves

finely grated zest of 1 lemon

1 teaspoon Dijon mustard

1/4 cup extra virgin olive oil

1 tablespoon lemon-infused olive oil

sea salt and freshly ground black pepper

1 Place chicken, bay leaf, onion and carrot in a large saucepan and completely cover with cold water. Cover and bring to the boil over a high heat. Reduce heat to a simmer and poach chicken for 1 hour. Remove to a large bowl to cool covered with the poaching liquid.

2 Once cold, break up chicken meat and discard bones. In a small bowl whisk dressing ingredients to combine. Mix the chicken meat with the dressing and serve on a bed of cos lettuce leaves.

Serves 6

+ my advice ... choose free-range or corn-fed chickens at the very least, or completely organically raised chickens whenever possible. This is better for the chickens, advantageous to the cook and good for the health of diners.

spiced couscous salad with lamb and feta

I've used Israeli couscous for this recipe, but if you can't find this giant version then ordinary couscous is just fine. If using ordinary couscous, follow the notes given here and adjust the liquid quantity.

600g lamb short-loins (sometimes called lamb back-straps)

1/4 cup olive oil

1 large onion, peeled and chopped

2 cloves garlic, crushed

1 teaspoon turmeric

1/2 teaspoon cinnamon powder

2 1/2 cups chicken stock

1 1/2 cups Israeli couscous (or substitute ordinary couscous and reduce stock to 1 1/2 cups)

150g feta cheese, crumbled

1/2 cup sun-dried tomatoes, chopped

2 red peppers, seeds removed, roasted, skinned and sliced

zest and juice of 1 lemon

3 tablespoons each, chopped fresh mint and parsley

sea salt and freshly ground black pepper

1 Cook lamb under a preheated grill or in a frying pan for 3–5 minutes on each side for medium-rare. Remove to rest and cool for 15 minutes, then thickly slice.

2 Heat a large saucepan, add oil and onion and cook over a medium heat for 5 minutes to lightly brown. Add crushed garlic, turmeric and cinnamon, and cook for 30 seconds, then add stock and bring to the boil. Stir in Israeli couscous, cover and simmer for 8–10 minutes, stirring occasionally until grains have softened.

Note: If using ordinary couscous, add couscous to the pan, remove pan from the heat, cover and leave to steam for 5–8 minutes to soften. Remove covering and fluff couscous with a fork.

3 Set couscous aside to cool. Toss sliced lamb and remaining salad ingredients with couscous to combine. Season well with salt and pepper to taste.

Serves 4

+ my favourite ... belongings are all related to cooking and serving food: new and old crockery, cutlery, cooking and serving bowls and tableware. It's silly to have lovely things sitting on display or hidden in a cupboard when using them gives so much pleasure.

mixed pepper penne salad with sun-dried tomato dressing

This dressing recipe makes quite a large amount, but it lasts for up to two weeks if stored in a screw-top jar in the fridge. Use it to dress other simple salads, such as avocado, poached chicken, potato or pasta salads.

350g penne pasta

1 quantity stewed mixed peppers (see page 43)

sun-dried tomato dressing

1/4 cup sun-dried tomatoes

3 tablespoons red wine vinegar

2 cloves garlic, peeled

1/2 teaspoon sugar

5–6 anchovies

1 tablespoon quality aged balsamic vinegar

1/4 cup extra virgin olive oil

sea salt and freshly ground black pepper

1 Cook penne pasta in plenty of boiling salted water according to packet instructions for about 12 minutes or until al dente (tender to the bite). Drain well and set aside to cool. Prepare stewed peppers and set aside to cool.
2 To make dressing, place sun-dried tomatoes in a bowl, heat red wine vinegar in a pan and pour over sun-dried tomatoes. Leave tomatoes to soften in hot vinegar for 30 minutes. Place all dressing ingredients in the bowl of a food processor and process to combine into a chunky-textured paste. Adjust seasoning with salt and pepper to taste.
3 In a large bowl, combine peppers with pasta and dressing to taste and toss well.

Serves 4-6

greek-style salad with creamed feta dressing

Greek salad is an all-time favourite of mine. Here I've tweaked it a little by creating a creamed feta dressing to dollop over the salad vegetables.

1 red pepper, halved, and seeds removed

1 telegraph cucumber, halved lengthways
   and seeds removed

1 cup red cherry tomatoes

9 medium-sized, ripe tomatoes, halved

1/2 cup Kalamata olives

sea salt and freshly ground black pepper

creamed feta dressing

1 cup plain yoghurt

200g feta cheese, crumbled

3 tablespoons chopped fresh basil

1 tablespoon chopped fresh mint

juice of 1 lemon

1 Slice pepper and cucumber into chunks and toss with cherry tomatoes, tomato halves and olives in a large serving bowl. Season with salt and pepper to taste.
2 In a small bowl, whisk dressing ingredients together until smooth.
3 Serve salad with dressing on the side to dollop on top of individual serves.

Serves 6

+ how to ... remove the seeds from a cucumber. Cut the cucumber in half lengthways and run a teaspoon down the length of the cucumber (cut-side up) to scrape out the central canal of seeds. Discard seeds and cut flesh as desired.

+ visual impact ... for a casual interactive approach, invest in some big white serving platters and let everyone help themselves from these.

warm roast chicken and white bean salad

You will need to think about preparing this salad the day before, as the beans need to soak overnight.

1 cup dried white beans (haricot, cannelini or baby Lima)

2 bay leaves

1 corn-fed, free-range chicken, rinsed and patted dry
   with paper towels

olive oil

sea salt and freshly ground black pepper

2 courgettes, trimmed

1 red onion, finely sliced

basil oil dressing

½ cup basil oil

2 cloves garlic, crushed

2 tablespoons white wine vinegar

¼ cup torn fresh basil leaves

1 Soak beans overnight in plenty of cold water. Next day, drain beans and place in a saucepan with the bay leaves and plenty of fresh cold water to cover. Bring to the boil, then turn down the heat and simmer for 1 hour until beans are tender. Drain well and place beans in a large bowl.

2 Meanwhile, place chicken in an oven pan, drizzle with olive oil and season with salt and pepper. Roast in an oven heated to 190°C for 1¼ hours or until juices run clear when a knife is inserted into the thickest part of the thigh. Remove to cool. Once cold enough to handle, remove chicken meat and discard the bones. Break flesh into bite-sized pieces and combine with cooked beans.

3 Shave courgettes into long thin strips with a vegetable peeler. Add courgettes and red onion to the salad bowl.

4 Combine dressing ingredients and pour over bean and chicken salad while still warm so that the flavours are well absorbed. Season with salt and pepper to taste. Serve as a warm salad or refrigerate to cool completely.

Serves 6

+ how to ... make basil oil. Remove the leaves from a large bunch of basil. Dunk the leaves briefly in boiling water to scald, then quickly plunge in ice-cold water to cool. Dry leaves well on paper towels. Place basil in a blender with twice as much olive oil and liquidise. Strain to remove pulp. Store infused oil in the fridge.

tuna, potato and green bean salad with olive tapanade dressing

Having quality canned tuna in the store-cupboard means you can easily and amply cater for unexpected company. I recommend Ortiz white tuna for its incomparable taste and texture.

800g washed baby potatoes

250g green beans, trimmed

220g quality canned tuna, drained and roughly flaked

1 cup red cherry tomatoes

2 red onions, finely sliced

olive tapenade dressing

1/4 cup parsley leaves, tightly packed

2 tablespoons salted capers, rinsed and drained

2 cloves garlic, peeled

1 cup pitted quality black olives

4 anchovies (optional)

juice of 1 lemon

1/3 cup extra virgin olive oil

sea salt and freshly ground black pepper

1 Cook potatoes in boiling salted water for about 10 minutes or until just tender. Drain and set aside to cool. Blanch beans in boiling salted water for 2–3 minutes until cooked to your liking. Drain beans and plunge into ice-cold water to cool completely and retain their vivid green colour. Drain again and set aside.

2 To make olive tapenade dressing, place parsley, capers and garlic in the bowl of a food processor and pulse until well chopped. Add olives, anchovies if desired and lemon juice and pulse to chop. With the motor running, add olive oil in a steady stream until amalgamated. Check and adjust seasoning with salt and pepper to taste.

3 Combine all salad ingredients in a large bowl. Pour over dressing, toss well and serve.

Serves 6

+ flavour options ... use the tapenade to dress other salads, or the separate components of this salad at different times. Serve baby potatoes with tapenade dressing one time; beans or tomatoes with tapenade the next.

+ my favourite ... anchovies are Ortiz anchovies, which are imported from northern Spain. These hand-filleted anchovies are firm-fleshed with a refined anchovy flavour and are like nothing you've ever tasted before.

mix and match old and new, plain and patterned and different coloured tableware items for an individualistic edge.

thai beef noodle salad

I recommend this salad as the consummate all-in-one light and fragrant meal for easy entertaining.

750g eye fillet of beef

300g egg noodles

2 carrots, peeled and finely grated

1/2 telegraph cucumber, seeds removed and finely sliced

1 cup mung bean sprouts

4 spring onions, finely sliced

1 cup mizuna lettuce or mesclun mix

1/4 cup torn fresh mint leaves

1/4 cup chopped fresh coriander

chilli garlic dressing

juice of 3 limes

2–3 tablespoons fish sauce

3 tablespoons palm sugar, or brown sugar

3 tablespoons water

1 small red chilli, seeds removed and finely chopped

2 cloves garlic, thinly sliced

1 Preheat oven to 220°C. Sear beef very quickly in a hot frying pan to brown, then place in an oven pan. Roast for 20 minutes for medium-rare. Remove to rest and cool, then slice thinly.

2 Cook noodles in plenty of boiling salted water for 2–3 minutes or according to packet instructions until just tender. Drain and splash with cold water to cool. Remove to a bowl to cool completely.

3 In a small bowl, whisk dressing ingredients together until sugar has dissolved. Adjust dressing to taste by adding a little extra of any ingredient to gain the perfect blend of sour, sweet, hot and salty flavours.

4 Combine remaining salad ingredients in the bowl with the cold noodles. Just before serving add sliced beef and pour over prepared dressing. Toss well and serve.

Serves 4

+ my favourite ... citrus juicer is a Mexican lime press. This device turns lime halves inside-out while pressing every last drop of juice out of often hard-to-squeeze limes, and it strains out the pips! I'd have to say that it's quite possibly the best kitchen tool I've ever invested in.

06 late

Pleasing combinations of great flavours.
Uncomplicated food to share with family
and friends. Start late and feast slowly
to prolong lunch until dinner time.

lunch

chicken and porcini pot pies

Dried porcini add a deliciously autumnal flavour to these pot pies.

15g dried porcini, soaked in 1/2 cup warm
   water for 20 minutes

olive oil

1 onion, peeled and chopped

400g button mushrooms, quartered

4 single, skinless, chicken breasts, cut into cubes

1/4 cup plain flour

1/2 cup red wine

1 cup chicken stock

3 tablespoons sour cream

2 tablespoons chopped fresh oregano

sea salt and freshly ground black pepper

3 pre-rolled sheets puff pastry

1 egg, lightly beaten with a pinch of salt, to glaze

1 Heat oil in a saucepan and cook onion and button mushrooms over a medium heat for 5–8 minutes until softened but not coloured, then remove to one side. Raise the heat, add the chicken to the pan and toss to lightly brown all over. This will need to be done in 2–3 batches, adding more oil if needed. Remove chicken to one side.
2 Remove pan from the heat and stir flour into remaining oil to form a smooth paste (add more oil if necessary to reach this consistency). Add the wine, strained porcini soaking liquid and stock, stirring to form a smooth sauce. Simmer for 5 minutes to cook flour. Stir in sour cream, oregano, porcini, onions, mushrooms, chicken, and season with salt and pepper to taste. Cool before spooning into 6 individual 1-cup capacity ramekins.
3 Cut pastry into 6 circles, 1cm larger than the circumference of the ramekins. Brush underside edges of pastry with beaten egg and fit lids to securely cover filling. Crimp pastry edges with a fork and cut a few small slits in the surface to release steam during cooking. Refrigerate for 30 minutes.
4 Preheat oven to 190°C. Glaze pastry lids with beaten egg. Bake for 30 minutes until pasty is puffed and golden brown. Serve immediately.

Serves 6

+ serving suggestion ... serve with a simple, green side salad dressed with quality extra virgin olive oil and a good splash of aged balsamic vinegar.

+ good idea ... **use a coffee filter to strain porcini soaking liquid of grit.**

moroccan chicken and apricot tagine

The caramel flavours of honey add depth to this fruity sauce.

6 chicken legs, drumstick and thigh separated

3 tablespoons olive oil

1 teaspoon each, ground cumin, turmeric and coriander

400g can chopped tomatoes

2 tablespoons liquid honey

1/2 cup dried apricots

1/2 cup pitted quality black olives

sea salt and freshly ground black pepper

1/4 cup toasted pine nuts

1/4 cup chopped fresh coriander or parsley

1 Preheat oven to 190°C. Heat a frying pan, add oil and brown chicken pieces for 1–2 minutes on both sides. Remove to a roasting pan.
2 In the same pan fry spices for 30 seconds, then add tomatoes, honey, apricots, and olives. Bring to the boil and season with salt and pepper, then pour sauce over chicken. Bake for 60–75 minutes, or until the juices of the chicken run clear when a sharp knife is inserted to the bone.
3 Serve chicken with a generous portion of sauce, scattered with pine nuts and fresh coriander or parsley.

Serves 6

+ serving suggestion ... serve this chicken tagine with a steamed green vegetable such as asparagus, broccoli or green beans, and with buttered couscous if desired.

char-grilled chicken with avocado salsa

I'll often cook this simply delicious dish when I'm home alone. The recipe is for four people but it's easy to divide everything by four – use the remaining half avocado on toast for breakfast the next day.

4 single, skinless, chicken breasts

2–3 tablespoons balsamic vinegar

2 tablespoons olive oil

sea salt and freshly ground black pepper

avocado salsa

2 avocados, halved, seeds removed and peeled

1 small red chilli, seeds removed and chopped

4 spring onions, finely sliced

1/4 cup salted capers, rinsed and drained

1/4 cup chopped fresh coriander

grated zest and juice of 2 limes (or lemons)

2 tablespoons avocado oil or extra virgin olive oil

sea salt and freshly ground black pepper

1 Brush the chicken breasts with balsamic vinegar and then olive oil and season with salt and pepper. Char-grill, barbecue, grill or fry chicken in a non-stick frying pan over a medium heat for 8–10 minutes on each side or until cooked through.
2 To make the avocado salsa, dice the avocado flesh and combine in a bowl with the remaining salsa ingredients. Season with salt and pepper and toss well.
3 Serve generous amounts of salsa over cooked chicken breasts.

Serves 4

+ searing meat is an important process as the high heat caramelises the natural sugars present in the meat. The burnt sugars turn brown, adding depth of colour and rich flavour to the completed dish. This works for every dish from plain steak to long-cooked stews.

grilled oriental eggplant with coriander noodles

Here are a great couple of dishes to serve to late lunch guests. The noodles can be completely prepared the day before, and the eggplant can marinate for as long as necessary and then be quickly grilled whenever you're ready.

9 long thin (Asian) eggplants, sliced in half lengthways

ginger soy marinade

½ cup light soy sauce

½ cup dry sherry

1 tablespoon sesame oil

2 cloves garlic, crushed

3cm piece ginger, peeled and finely grated

2 tablespoons sesame seeds, toasted

coriander noodles

3 cloves garlic, peeled

2cm piece fresh ginger, peeled

pinch chilli powder

1 cup fresh coriander leaves, tightly packed

¼ cup peanut oil

sea salt and freshly ground black pepper

400g egg noodles

1 Place sliced eggplant in a large, shallow, non-metallic dish. Combine marinade ingredients, except sesame seeds, in a saucepan and bring to the boil. Strain marinade over eggplant and leave to marinate for at least 4 hours or overnight in the fridge.

2 When ready to cook eggplant, preheat grill on high. Drain eggplant and place on grill rack. Grill for 3 minutes on each side, brushing with marinade to moisten. Sprinkle with sesame seeds and serve with coriander noodles on the side.

3 To prepare the coriander noodles, combine noodle dressing ingredients in the bowl of a food processor and process to form a smooth paste. Season with salt and pepper to taste.

4 Cook noodles in boiling salted water for 2–3 minutes or according to packet instructions. Drain and toss with dressing in a bowl. Refrigerate to chill before serving.

Serves 6

+ my advice ... though this is not always the case, judge chillies by a rule of thumb that says the smaller the chilli, the more intense the heat. Remove the seeds and membranes to reduce the heat factor if preferred.

+ visual impact ... plan the way you want the food to look when plated-up; present all serving portions in the same formation so that they are stamped with café-style expertise.

green tea noodle bowl with barbecue duck

Invite friends to a steam boat lunch and have them dip their own collection of these ingredients in the steaming hot, aromatic broth.

225g packet green tea noodles

1 bunch baby bok choy, trimmed and blanched

1.5 litres chicken stock

3cm piece fresh ginger, peeled and finely sliced

1 small red chilli, finely chopped

1 Chinese barbecue duck, chopped in pieces
   (the store chef will do this for you)

100g enoki mushrooms

1 Cook noodles in boiling salted water for 2 minutes. Drain well and set aside. Blanch bok choy in boiling salted water for 1 minute, then plunge into ice-cold water to refresh. Drain and set aside.

2 Place chicken stock, ginger and chilli in a saucepan and bring to the boil, then simmer for 10 minutes for flavours to infuse.

3 Strain to remove flavourings and return stock to the pan. Add duck and simmer for 2–3 minutes to heat through. Add noodles, bok choy and enoki mushrooms and simmer for 2–3 minutes more. Serve in deep bowls.

Serves 4-6

+ shortcut ... ask the chef at your local Asian food market to chop the Chinese barbecue duck into pieces for you – it will be done expertly and with ease. Go shopping and stock up on Asian store-cupboard ingredients while you wait.

hokkien noodles with pork and spinach

Hokkien noodles are my most favourite type of thick noodle. They cook instantly and have a fabulous slippery-soft, mouth-filling texture.

vegetable oil

500g pork mince

600g Hokkien noodles (soak in a bowl of
   boiling water for 1 minute)

150g baby spinach leaves

1/4 cup light soy sauce (or more to taste)

1/4 cup Thai sweet chilli sauce (or more to taste)

1/2 cup toasted cashew nuts

1 Heat a wok or large frying pan, add a little oil, then add pork mince and stir-fry over a high heat for about 5–6 minutes until separated and well browned.

2 Drain noodles, add to pan with spinach and sauces to taste. Toss and stir-fry over high heat for 5 minutes for noodles to heat through and spinach to wilt. Scatter with cashew nuts and serve immediately.

Serves 4

+ shortcut ... buy ready-roasted and salted cashew nuts to complete this dish. The wonderful waxy crunch of cashews is the perfect textural contrast to the softness of the Hokkien noodles.

+ how to ... cook en papillote. En papillote is the French term for when food is baked inside a wrapping of parchment paper. As the food cooks it emits steam and the paper puffs up. At the table, the paper is opened to reveal the succulent steamed food.

fish and pasta in paper

I picked up this clever idea in my travels. Even though it may seem unusual to cook pasta in paper, I can confirm that it works very well.

350g fettuccine, linguine or spaghetti

¼ cup olive oil

2 cloves garlic, chopped

400g can chopped tomatoes

½ cup chicken stock

¼ cup torn fresh basil leaves

sea salt and freshly ground black pepper

400g raw prawns, peeled with tails intact, de-veined

400g firm-fleshed, white fish fillets, for example snapper or cod, cubed

4 large sheets greaseproof or non-stick baking paper

1 Cook pasta in plenty of boiling, salted water for 8–10 minutes or until just under-cooked. Drain well.

2 Make a simple tomato sauce. Heat a saucepan, add oil and garlic and cook for 30 seconds over a medium heat. Add canned tomatoes and stock and simmer, stirring regularly for 5 minutes (the sauce will be quite wet). Stir in basil and season with salt and pepper.

3 Preheat oven to 200°C. Combine pasta, fish, prawns and tomato sauce in a bowl and mix well. Lay sheets of paper over bowls for ease of assembly. Divide mixture between sheets of paper, making sure they are well moistened with sauce. Securely wrap parcels to enclose filling by folding over edges of paper several times or twisting edges together at the top.

4 Bake for 15 minutes or until prawns are cooked. Serve immediately in the paper parcel to contain the cooking juices.

Serves 4

tamarind prawn and cellophane noodle stir-fry

Stir-fries are excellent impromptu dishes to throw together if people arrive unexpectedly and stay on for a meal. Keep a variety of noodles and Asian sauces in the store-cupboard as a base, then make substitutions for other ingredients if necessary.

300g bean thread cellophane noodles (sometimes called rice vermicelli)

3 tablespoons peanut or canola oil

4cm piece fresh ginger, finely grated

20 raw prawns, peeled with tails intact, de-veined

2–3 tablespoons liquid honey

3–4 tablespoons tamarind water

2–3 tablespoons fish sauce

500g Asian greens, trimmed, such as bok choy, Chinese broccoli, choy sum

1 Soak cellophane noodles in cold water for 5 minutes to soften, then cook in boiling water for 2–3 minutes and drain well.

2 Heat oil in a wok or large frying pan, add ginger and prawns and stir-fry for 1 minute. Raise the heat, add honey, tamarind water, fish sauce and Asian greens and stir-fry quickly until greens are wilted.

3 Toss in hot noodles and stir-fry for a few minutes to heat through. Serve immediately.

Serves 4

+ good idea ... get to know Asian greens as they are plentiful, inexpensive and nutritious. Start with readily accessible gai lan (Chinese broccoli), bok choy (Chinese white cabbage), and choy sum (flowering Chinese cabbage).

italian mashed potato pie

This recipe is adapted from my friend Raffaela Delmonte's authentic rendition that appears in her charming book, *The Fragrance of Basil* (Penguin).

butter to grease tin

3 tablespoons dried breadcrumbs

1.5kg floury potatoes, peeled and roughly chopped

¼ cup extra virgin olive oil

¼ cup warmed milk

1 egg, lightly beaten

½ cup grated fresh Parmesan cheese

sea salt and freshly ground black pepper

150g feta cheese, crumbled

100g chorizo or salami, roughly chopped (optional)

¼ cup chopped fresh parsley

½ cup pitted black olives

½ cup semi-dried tomatoes

2 tablespoons capers, rinsed and drained

25g butter, cut in small cubes

1 Preheat oven to 190°C. Grease a 24cm springform cake tin with butter and dust with 2 tablespoons dried breadcrumbs.

2 Cook potatoes in boiling, salted water until tender. Drain well and briefly return saucepan to the heat to drive out as much moisture as possible from the potatoes. Mash potatoes or put through a potato ricer. Beat in olive oil, milk, egg and Parmesan. Season with salt and pepper to taste.

3 Spread half the mashed potato mixture into the base of the tin. Scatter with feta, chorizo or salami (if desired) and parsley. Top with remaining potato. Arrange olives, semi-dried tomatoes and capers on top of the cake. Finish by sprinkling the remaining tablespoon of breadcrumbs on top and dot the surface with butter.

4 Bake for 30–40 minutes or until golden brown. Cool a little before removing from tin. Slice in wedges to serve.

Serves 8

+ flavour option ... omit chorizo or salami for a vegetarian version.

+ my favourite ... grating tool is a Microplane™, which makes light work of turning hard-to-grate food items into delicate flakes. This tool is excellent for finely grating Parmesan and chocolate, cleanly cutting through the fibres of fresh root ginger, and removing the zest from citrus fruits just like magic without taking any of the white pith.

green fish curry

I'm very pleased with my rendition of this classic green fish curry. Served with fragrant jasmine rice, it is just perfection.

5cm piece fresh ginger, peeled

2 cloves garlic

3 spring onions, chopped

1 green chilli, seeds removed

3 tablespoons chopped fresh coriander

2 fresh kaffir lime leaves, roughly chopped

2 tablespoons canola oil

800g white-fleshed fish, such as snapper or cod

400ml can light coconut milk

sea salt

fresh limes, halved

1 Place ginger, garlic, spring onions, chilli, coriander, kaffir leaves and oil in a food processor and blend to form a green curry paste. Cut fish into 3cm cubes.

2 Place coconut milk in a large saucepan and bring to the boil. Simmer to reduce by half. Stir in curry paste.

3 Place cubed fish in sauce and simmer very gently for 5 minutes to cook through. Season with salt to taste. Serve with steamed jasmine rice and fresh lime halves on the side for squeezing over fish.

Serves 4

+ shortcut ... if you find handling chillies unpleasant, try pressing them through a garlic crusher instead of chopping them by hand. The garlic press will crush a chilli to a paste.

mum's fish cakes

My mum, Loraine, makes the most memorable fish cakes I've ever tasted and this is close to her recipe. As she is a natural and instinctively good cook, it's hard to say exactly!

500g floury potatoes

2 tablespoons butter, melted

500g white-fleshed fish fillets, for example snapper or cod

1 cup milk

1 small onion, finely chopped

2 tablespoons chopped parsley

sea salt and freshly ground black pepper

1/2 cup plain flour

1 egg, beaten

1 tablespoon milk

2 cups dry breadcrumbs

1 Cook potatoes in boiling, salted water until tender. Drain well and mash with melted butter, then cool. Place fish fillets in a large saucepan and cover with milk. Cook over a gentle heat for 8 minutes. Remove to cool in cooking liquid.

2 Drain and break fish fillets into small pieces and combine with potato, onion and parsley. Season well with salt and pepper. Form mixture into 8 thick patties.

3 Spread flour on a tray. Beat egg and milk together in a bowl and spread breadcrumbs out on another tray. Dip patties in flour, then egg and then crumbs to coat.

4 Heat a frying pan with a little olive oil and gently fry fish cakes over a medium heat for 3–4 minutes on each side until golden brown.

Makes 8

+ substitute ... flaked smoked fish, hot-smoked salmon or canned tuna can all be used in this recipe to create different flavour effects.

salmon and courgette flans

These are rich little numbers but seductively so! Make them as an extra special treat when you have a select few visitors for lunch.

butter or oil to grease ramekins

4 eggs

4 egg yolks

3/4 cup cream

3/4 cup milk

100g smoked salmon, roughly chopped

1 courgette, trimmed and grated

3/4 cup grated Gruyère cheese

3 tablespoons finely chopped fresh chives

sea salt and freshly ground black pepper

1 Preheat oven to 175°C. Grease 4 1½-cup capacity ramekins.

2 Combine eggs and egg yolks in a large bowl and whisk lightly. Whisk in cream and milk to combine. Stir in salmon, grated courgette, cheese and chives and season with salt and pepper.

3 Pour mixture into prepared ramekins, evenly distributing the salmon, courgette and cheese between the ramekins. Place ramekins in an oven pan and fill pan with hot water to come half-way up the sides of the ramekins. Bake flans in this water bath for 35–40 minutes or until just set.

4 Run a small knife around the edge of each flan and invert ramekin to release flans. Serve warm.

Makes 4

+ serving suggestion ... depending on how hungry you and your guests are, serve one or all of the side salad selections featured on pages 108–109 with these flans.

fennel sausage and red wine risotto

When I say Italian risotto rice, I leave it open for you to choose between Carnaroli, Vialone Nano or Arborio.

600g coarse-textured, Italian-style fennel sausages, par-boiled for 2–3 minutes

3–4 tablespoons olive oil

1 onion, finely diced

3 cloves garlic, crushed

2 cups Italian risotto rice

1½ cups red wine

3–4 cups quality chicken stock, heated

3 tablespoons chopped fresh sage

sea salt and freshly ground black pepper

shaved fresh Parmesan cheese

1 In a frying pan with a little oil, brown sausages all over. Remove, thickly slice then set aside. In a saucepan bring stock to the boil, then simmer.

2 Heat a large heavy-based pan, add oil, then onion and garlic and sweat over a medium heat for 5–10 minutes until soft but not coloured. Add risotto rice and stir for 2 minutes to toast but not brown. Add the red wine to the pan and stir until this evaporates.

3 Add a ladleful of hot stock and stir until the mix is nearly dry, then repeat, adding stock until it is all absorbed and the rice is tender to the bite; this takes 15–20 minutes.

4 Stir in prepared sausages and sage, and season with salt and pepper to taste. Remove pan from the heat, cover with lid and leave to steam for 5 minutes. Stir through a little extra hot stock if necessary to create a creamy consistency. Serve topped with shaved Parmesan.

Serves 6

lemony ricotta, eggplant layers

This brilliant way of poaching eggplant was taught to me by my cousin Patty who lives in Italy. Poaching the eggplant in water eliminates its thirst for oil and leaves it incredibly moist, succulent and fat-free.

2 medium eggplants, sliced into 1cm thick rounds

1 cup ricotta

1 egg, lightly beaten

finely grated zest of 1 lemon

sea salt and freshly ground black pepper

2 roasted red peppers, thickly sliced

8 anchovies (optional)

1 Poach eggplant slices in simmering, salted water for 5 minutes until softened. Drain well.

2 Mix ricotta with egg and lemon zest, and season with salt and pepper to taste.

3 Lightly oil a baking dish and layer ingredients as for moussaka, or form individual layered stacks. Start with eggplant, spoon over a little ricotta mix, cover with some red pepper and an anchovy, then repeat layers until mixture is used up.

4 Bake at 200°C for 25 minutes or until golden brown.

Serves 4

+ shortcut ... slice eggplant with a serrated knife and not a regular chef's knife. The serration cuts through the sometimes tough skin of eggplants with ease.

haloumi with ratatouille

Haloumi is a traditional Cypriot-style stretched curd cheese that is stored in brine. It can be eaten raw, but in my opinion is best served grilled or fried.

¼ cup olive oil

1 large onion, peeled and diced

1 medium (350g) eggplant, cut into 1cm cubes

2 courgettes, cut into 1cm cubes

1 red pepper, seeds removed and diced

400g can chopped tomatoes

2 teaspoons raw sugar

2 tablespoons chopped fresh oregano

sea salt and freshly ground black pepper

500g haloumi

extra olive oil

fresh basil leaves to garnish

1 Heat a heavy-based pan, add oil and cook diced onion, eggplant, courgettes and pepper in 2–3 batches, tossing regularly for 4–5 minutes until golden brown.

2 Return all vegetables to the pan. Add canned tomatoes and sugar and bring to the boil, then turn down the heat and gently simmer for 15 minutes, stirring regularly. Stir in oregano and season with salt and pepper to taste.

3 Cut haloumi into four slices. Heat a grill or frying pan with a little oil and cook haloumi for 2–3 minutes on each side until golden brown.

4 Serve ratatouille with one slice of haloumi per person, placed at a jaunty angle, and garnished with basil leaves.

Serves 4

+ serving suggestion ... serve ratatouille with crusty bread to mop up the juices.

+ my advice ... to achieve a true gauge of flavour, it is best to season long-cooked dishes with salt and pepper towards the end of cooking. Pepper loses flavour during long cooking and can sometimes impart a bitterness; salt is concentrated by reduction during cooking time.

+ visual impact ... presentation is very important. Create visually impressive dishes by achieving some height on the plate wherever possible (without being ridiculous). Build meals by layering components, such as placing the main ingredient on top of the vegetables, salad or starch accompaniments.

07.aft

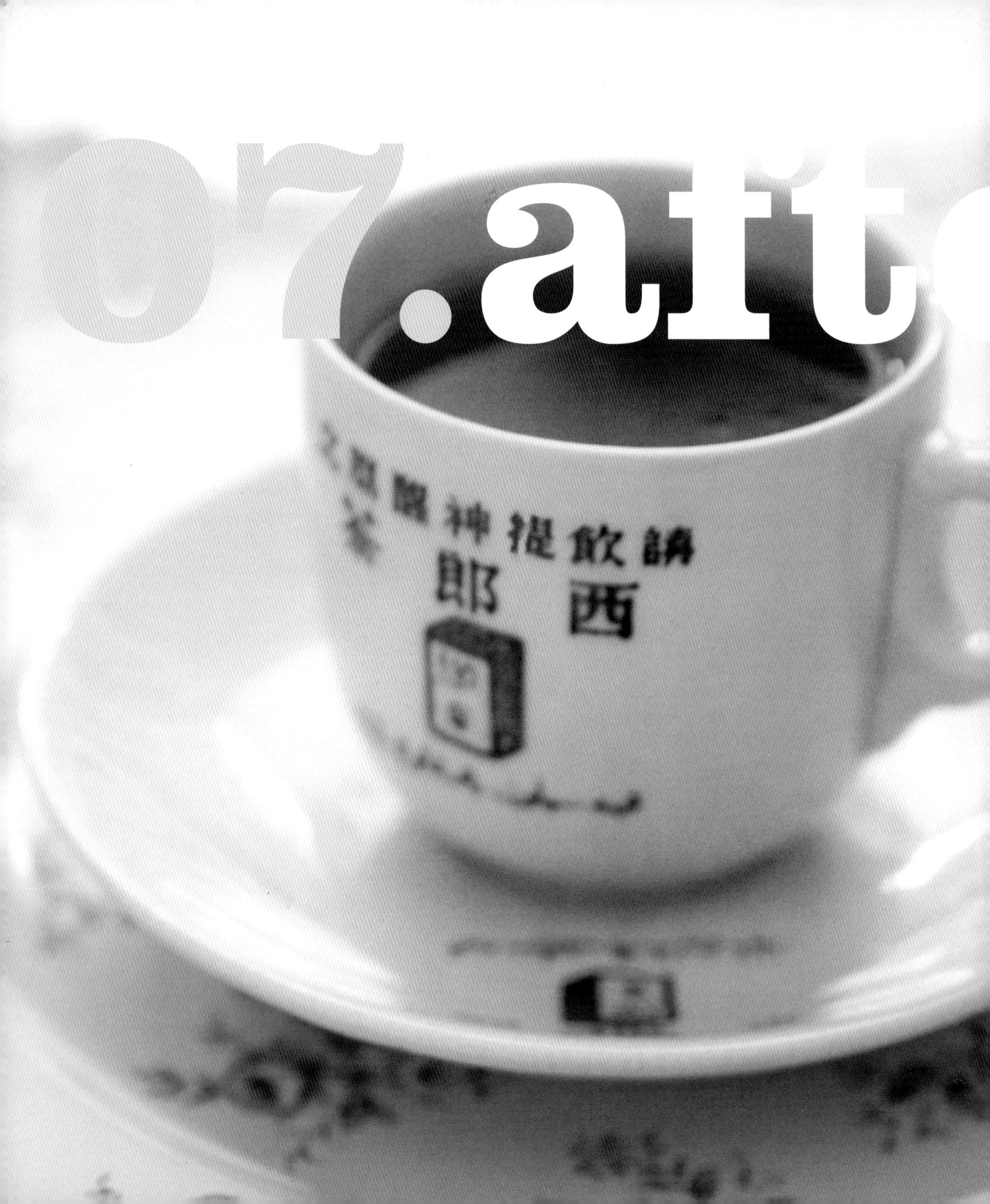

ernoo
tea

Magical sweet delights. Revive forgotten pleasures: tea-sets, the tea cosy, pretty plates, mix-and-match napkins. Special treats to celebrate family and friends.

masala chai

Senses are soothed with beguiling perfumes and flavours present in this exotic tea infusion.

1 teaspoon each whole coriander seeds, allspice berries,
   cardamom pods
1 cinnamon stick
1 litre water
2 tablespoons Darjeeling tea leaves
milk
sugar to taste

1 Place all spices and water in a large saucepan and bring to the boil, then simmer, covered, for 10 minutes to extract flavours. Add tea leaves and steep for 3 minutes. Strain into a jug.
2 Add milk, and sugar to taste if desired.

Makes 4 cups

moroccan mint tea

This is a natural herbal infusion made with the invigorating qualities of mint.

several sprigs fresh mint
1 teaspoon sugar, or more to taste
boiling water

1 Place mint in a heatproof glass or cup. Add sugar, and with a teaspoon gently crush sugar into the mint to release its essential flavours.
2 Pour over enough boiling water to cover and leave to steep for 1 minute before drinking.

Serves 1

iced peach tea

Sipped slowly on a hot summer's day, this fruity iced tea is ambrosial.

3 floral herbal tea bags, such as rosehip
1.5 litres boiling water
1/4–1/2 cup sugar to taste
1 cup peach nectar (or puréed peaches)
3 fresh peaches, sliced
1/4 telegraph cucumber, seeds removed and sliced
fresh mint leaves
ice cubes to serve

1 Place tea bags in a heatproof jug and pour over boiling water. Leave tea to steep for 5 minutes, then remove tea bags. Stir in sugar to sweeten to taste. Set aside to cool.
2 Stir in peach nectar, peach slices and cucumber, and chill well. Add ice cubes and fresh mint leaves to serve.

Serves 4-6

+ tisanes (herbal tea infusions) have been drunk for centuries, both for their refreshing qualities and for medicinal purposes.

herbal tea infusions can be made from almost any edible plant or flower. Simply add boiling water to 2 tablespoons of fresh herbs per cup. Infuse for a few minutes then remove herbs; sweeten with honey if desired.

ribbon tea sandwiches

Here are some filling ideas for layered sandwiches, which are sliced in ribbons for a dainty savoury sandwich snack at afternoon tea time. I like to use a variety of different sliced sandwich bread such as white, multi-grain and wholegrain.

green pesto (see page 22) layer, with a second layer of
   olive tapenade (see page 117)
sliced smoked salmon, with a mixture of cream cheese,
   capers and chopped fresh dill
red pesto (see page 22), with sliced pastrami
   and rocket leaves
egg salad (see opposite), with very finely sliced cucumber

1 Spread filling to the edges of each slice of bread. Top with second slice of bread. Spread with second filling of choice and top with another slice of bread. If the fillings are moist then there is no need to butter the bread, unless butter or mayonnaise is preferred.
2 Remove crusts from all sides of stack and slice into 3 long ribbon sandwiches.

Makes 3 or more

egg salad sandwich spread

The simplicity of a filling like this reminds us that honest food is hard to beat.

4 large eggs
20g butter, softened
2–3 tablespoons chopped fresh parsley, chives or chervil
1 teaspoon Dijon mustard
1/4 cup mayonnaise (preferably homemade)
sea salt and freshly ground black pepper

1 Place eggs in a saucepan of cold water to cover. Bring water to the boil, then time the cooking of eggs for 6 minutes. Remove and plunge into ice-cold water to cool.
2 Peel off egg shells, place eggs in a bowl and mash with a fork. Stir in remaining ingredients and season with salt and pepper to taste.

Makes enough filling for 5-6 sandwiches

+ visual impact ... give all plates the polish of a professional kitchen by paying attention to garnishes and make sure these are simple but uniform, such as a small piece of dill, which always works well with fish.

+ good idea ... use a hot
and slightly moist knife to
cut this slice as it is of a
sticky consistency. Dip the
knife in hot water and
loosely wipe with a clean
cloth between cuts.

blueberry and cranberry lemon shortcake

I love the layered effect of this pretty slice. Due to its alluring charm, I recommend serving it cut into small squares.

1½ cups blueberries (fresh or frozen)
1½ cups dried cranberries (equals 1 packet 'Craisins')
2 cups water

shortcake

½ cup caster sugar
1½ cups plain flour
200g cold butter, cubed

lemon topping

2 large eggs
¾ cup sugar
juice and finely grated zest of 3 lemons
¼ cup plain flour
icing sugar to dust

1 Combine blueberries, cranberries and water in a saucepan and simmer gently for about 30 minutes until cranberries are soft and pulpy and water has been completely absorbed. Watch carefully, and stir regularly while cooking. Set aside to cool.
2 Preheat oven to 200°C. Line a 20cm square cake tin with non-stick bakng paper to come up the sides. Place caster sugar, flour and butter in the bowl of a food processor and process until crumbly. Press mixture into base of tin. Bake for 15–20 minutes or until golden brown. Spread cold blueberry and cranberry purée over cooked crust. Reduce oven temperature to 160°C.
3 To make lemon topping, beat eggs and sugar until thick and pale. Beat in lemon juice and zest and ¼ cup plain flour. Pour over berry shortcake and bake for 45–50 minutes or until set.
4 Cool, then remove from tin by lifting paper and chill well. Cut into small squares and serve dusted with icing sugar.

Makes 36

louise cake tartlets

These tartlets are just the thing to complement a nice cup of tea.

pastry

1 cup plain flour

1/2 cup icing sugar

pinch salt

125g butter, roughly cubed

1 tablespoon cold water

filling

1/2 cup raspberry jam

2 egg whites

1/2 cup caster sugar

1/2 cup fine desiccated coconut

1 Place flour, icing sugar and salt in the bowl of a food processor and pulse to sift. Add cubed butter and process until crumbly. Add water and process just until the mixture forms a ball of pastry.

2 Lightly grease a 24-hole mini muffin pan with butter or spray with oil. Divide the pastry into 24 even pieces and press into prepared pans to form 24 pastry cases. Refrigerate for 30 minutes.

3 Preheat oven to 180°C. Place 1 teaspoonful of jam in each pastry case. In a bowl whisk egg whites until stiff peaks form. Gradually add sugar while whisking continuously. Fold in coconut. Divide this mixture between the tartlets, spooning 1–2 teaspoonfuls on top of jam centres.

4 Bake for 25 minutes. Cool a little in tins to firm before removing to a wire rack.

Makes 24

+ my advice ... **to preserve the flavour of loose-leaf tea, it is best stored at room temperature in an airtight and lightproof container.**

mango cup-cakes

+ my favourite ... tradition is the ritual of afternoon tea. I like to use nice china tea cups, select a favourite tea and leave it to steep in a pot covered with a pretty tea cosy. Sharing tea and conversation is always memorable.

mango cup-cakes

Mango adds a subtle scented taste of the exotic to these cup-cakes.

1 fresh mango, peeled and flesh removed from stone

125g butter, softened

3/4 cup caster sugar

finely grated zest of 1 lemon

3 eggs

1/2 cup yoghurt

1 cup plain flour

1 teaspoon baking powder

mango icing

25g softened butter

2 cups icing sugar

1/2 mango purée (reserved from cup-cake mixture)

1 cup shaved desiccated coconut

1 Preheat oven to 160°C on fan-bake. Lightly grease 12 individual, 3/4-cup capacity, cup-cake pans or line a standard muffin pan with cup-cake paper cases. Purée the mango flesh in a food processor.

2 In a bowl beat butter and sugar with an electric mixer until pale and creamy. Beat in lemon zest and eggs, then beat in half the mango purée (reserve the other half for the icing) and the yoghurt. Fold in sifted dry ingredients.

3 Pour into prepared pan or paper cases. Bake for 20 minutes or until a skewer inserted comes out clean. Remove to a rack to cool.

4 To make icing, place butter, icing sugar and mango purée in a bowl and beat well to combine and form a smooth creamy icing. Slather on top of cup-cakes and scatter with shaved coconut.

Makes 12

+ substitute ... canned mangoes if fresh mangoes are unavailable. An equivalent measurement is 1 fresh mango puréed equals 1 1/3 cups drained and puréed canned mango.

cherry chocolate meringue nests

Cherries are particularly suited to fill these tiny nests of meringue but other small fruits, such as berries, also work well.

2 egg whites

1/2 cup caster sugar

pinch cream of tartar

1 tablespoon Dutch process cocoa powder

1/2 cup mascarpone

26 fresh cherries (or substitute berries)

icing sugar to dust

1 Preheat oven to 100°C. Line 2 baking trays with non-stick baking paper.

2 Place egg whites, sugar and cream of tartar in a heat-proof bowl set over a pan of simmering water and whisk with an electric mixer for about 3–5 minutes until sugar has dissolved and mixture is warm. Remove bowl from heat and whisk for about 10 minutes until mixture is cold, stiff and glossy. Sift in cocoa powder and whisk briefly to incorporate.

3 Place mixture in a piping bag fitted with a wide nozzle and pipe even-sized 2cm round nests onto prepared trays. Bake for 1 hour until meringue is dry.

4 Remove to a wire rack to cool. Once cold, fill nests with a teaspoonful of mascarpone, top with a cherry and dust with icing sugar to serve.

Makes 26

+ good idea ... place leftover egg whites in a clean, dry container, cover and store in the fridge for up to 10 days. Alternatively, containers of egg whites can be frozen for up to 6 months. Defrost to room temperature before using in baking. To use in recipes, 30mls is equivalent to 1 egg white.

jaffa fudge cake

This makes an excellent celebration cake.

³/₄ cup cold water

finely grated zest and juice of 2 oranges

2 drops orange essence

250g butter, roughly cubed

2 cups caster sugar

200g quality dark cooking chocolate

1¹/₂ cups plain flour

¹/₄ cup Dutch process cocoa powder

2 eggs, lightly beaten

jaffa icing

1 cup roughly chopped, quality dark chocolate

1 cup cream

2–3 drops orange essence

zest of 1 orange, cut into fine strips

1 Preheat oven to 175°C on fan-bake. Line the base of a 22cm springform cake tin with non-stick baking paper, then grease and lightly flour the sides of the tin.

2 Combine water, zest, juice, essence, butter, sugar and chocolate in a saucepan. Heat gently until chocolate has melted and sugar has dissolved. Remove pan from the heat and allow mixture to cool slightly. Carefully whisk in sifted flour and cocoa. Stir in beaten eggs and pour into prepared tin. Bake for 1¹/₄ hours. Allow to cool before removing from tin.

3 To make icing, place chocolate, cream and essence in a bowl to melt over a saucepan of simmering water, stirring until smooth, or microwave. Remove to cool and thicken, then spread icing over cold cake. Decorate with orange zest strips if desired. Slice in wedges with a hot knife.

Serves 12

+ my advice ... take care during the process of melting chocolate because if chocolate comes into contact with steam or water it will 'seize', becoming granular, solid and impossible to work with. It will then have to be discarded.

+ my advice … **for best results, pour hot syrup over a cold cake or cold syrup over a hot cake so that the cake absorbs the syrup without becoming sodden.**

plum, coconut and lemon syrup cake

This is a heavenly cake, stained with dark plums and drenched in a lemon syrup. I've made it as a birthday cake and for afternoon tea, plus it can also double as an outstanding dessert.

225g butter, softened

1¼ cups caster sugar

4 small eggs

1½ cups fine desiccated coconut

1¼ cups plain flour

1½ teaspoons baking powder

8 fresh plums, halved and stones removed

lemon syrup

pared rind of 2 lemons

juice of 6 lemons

½ cup water

1 cup sugar

1 Preheat oven to 175°C on fan-bake. Grease and lightly dust a 22cm springform cake tin with flour.

2 In a bowl beat butter and sugar with an electric mixer until pale and creamy. Beat in eggs one at a time. Stir in coconut and sifted flour and baking powder. Pour mixture into prepared cake tin. Arrange halved plums over the surface of the cake.

3 Bake for 1 hour or until a skewer inserted comes out clean. Cool cake in the tin. Once cold, remove from the tin and pour over warm lemon syrup. Slice in wedges to serve.

4 To make lemon syrup, combine all ingredients in a saucepan. Bring to the boil, then simmer for 2 minutes until syrupy.

Serves 10-12

coconut cream loaf with pink icing

Different forms of coconut – desiccated, essence and cream – combine to intensify the flavour of this simple loaf.

125g butter

1 cup sugar

2 eggs

1/2 teaspoon coconut essence

3/4 cup coconut cream

1 1/2 cups self-raising flour

3/4 cup desiccated coconut

2 tablespoons shaved desiccated coconut to decorate

1 Preheat oven to 175°C. Grease and lightly dust a 21 x 11 x 6cm loaf tin with flour.
2 In a bowl beat butter and sugar with an electric mixer until pale and creamy. Beat in eggs, one at a time. Add coconut essence and coconut cream and beat to incorporate. Stir in flour and coconut.
3 Spoon into prepared loaf tin and bake for 45 minutes or until a skewer inserted comes out clean. Remove to a wire rack to cool. Once cold, drizzle with pink icing, decorate with shaved coconut and slice to serve.

Makes 1 loaf

+ how to make ... **pink icing: add 1–2 drops red food colouring to lemon icing (see nonettes page 73).**

chocolate macaroons

Macaroons have a marvellous chewy texture that is, in my opinion, unrivalled.

1/2 cup egg whites

1 1/4 cups caster sugar

1 tablespoon honey

1 teaspoon vanilla extract

2 3/4 cups fine desiccated coconut

1/2 cup Dutch process cocoa powder

1/4 cup plain flour

1 Heat oven to 160°C on fan-bake. Lightly grease a baking tray or line with non-stick baking paper.
2 In a bowl set over a pan of simmering water, whisk egg whites, sugar, honey and vanilla until mixture is very pale and sugar has dissolved (about 5 minutes). Remove from heat, stir in coconut, cocoa and flour sifted together. Chill until firm.
3 Shape into 30 balls and place on prepared baking tray. Bake for 25 minutes. Remove to a wire rack to cool.

Makes 30

+ **egg whites can be frozen in pottles for up to 6 months. Bring to room temperature before using in baking. These egg whites whip better than fresh ones, resulting in greater volume.**

chocolate almond thumbprints

This divinely rich, chocolate biscuit recipe of mine first appeared in *Cuisine* magazine.

1 tablespoon olive oil

3 tablespoons Dutch process cocoa powder

125g butter, softened

1/2 cup caster sugar

1 egg, separated

1 cup plain flour

1/2 cup (70g) almonds, finely ground in a food processor

100g dark chocolate, roughly chopped

3 tablespoons liquid cream

1 Heat oven to 180°C. Line a baking tray with non-stick baking paper.

2 Combine oil and cocoa in a small bowl. In a large bowl, beat butter and sugar with an electric mixer until creamy. Beat in egg yolk, then cocoa and oil mixture. Stir in flour to combine.

3 Place ground almonds in a bowl and lightly beaten egg white in another bowl. Divide dough into 20 even pieces and roll into balls. Dip each ball in egg white and then roll in ground almonds. Place on prepared oven tray, allowing space for biscuits to spread. Use your thumb to press a deep indentation into each ball. Bake for 10–12 minutes, until just set. Remove biscuits to a wire rack to cool.

4 Combine chocolate and cream in a bowl and melt over a pan of simmering water or carefully microwave, stirring until smooth. Spoon a little chocolate mixture into the centre of each biscuit and allow to set.

Makes 20

orange magdalenas

These enchantingly simple, oil-based, sponge cakes are ubiquitous throughout Spain. I became addicted to them during my travels there.

3 eggs

1/4 cup caster sugar

finely grated zest of 1 orange

1/2 cup plain flour, sifted

1/4 cup fruity olive oil

2 tablespoons milk

1 Preheat oven to 190°C on fan-bake. Grease 8 1/2-cup capacity cake tins or 12 mini muffin tins.

2 Place eggs, sugar and orange zest in a large bowl and whisk with an electric mixer until very pale and thick. Fold in flour with a metal spoon, then carefully fold in oil and milk to combine.

3 Spoon mixture into prepared tins and bake for 15–20 minutes (depending on size) or until firm and golden brown.

Makes 8–12

+ flavour options ... plain magdalenas are traditional. However, I find that the freshness of citrus works beautifully with the buttery flavour of olive oil. Try lemon or lime zest for a change.

index

PENGUIN BOOKS

Published by the Penguin Group

Penguin Books (NZ) Ltd, cnr Airborne and Rosedale Roads,
Albany, Auckland 1310, New Zealand
Penguin Books Ltd, 80 Strand,
London, WC2R 0RL, England
Penguin Group (USA) Inc., 375 Hudson Street,
New York, NY 10014, United States
Penguin Books Australia Ltd, 250 Camberwell Road, Camberwell,
Victoria 3124, Australia
Penguin Books Canada Ltd, 10 Alcorn Avenue,
Toronto, Ontario, Canada M4V 3B2
Penguin Books (South Africa) (Pty) Ltd, 24 Sturdee Avenue,
Rosebank, Johannesburg 2196, South Africa
Penguin Books India (P) Ltd, 11, Community Centre, Panchsheel
Park, New Delhi 110 017, India

Penguin Books Ltd, Registered Offices: 80 Strand,
London, WC2R 0RL, England

First published by Penguin Books (NZ) Ltd, 2003

1 3 5 7 9 10 8 6 4 2

Food photography by Bruce Nicholson. Incidental photography
by Julie Le Clerc
Designed and typeset by Athena Sommerfeld
Prepress by microdot
Printed in China through Bookbuilders

ISBN 0 14 301885 X
A catalogue record for this book is available from the National
Library of New Zealand.

www.penguin.co.nz